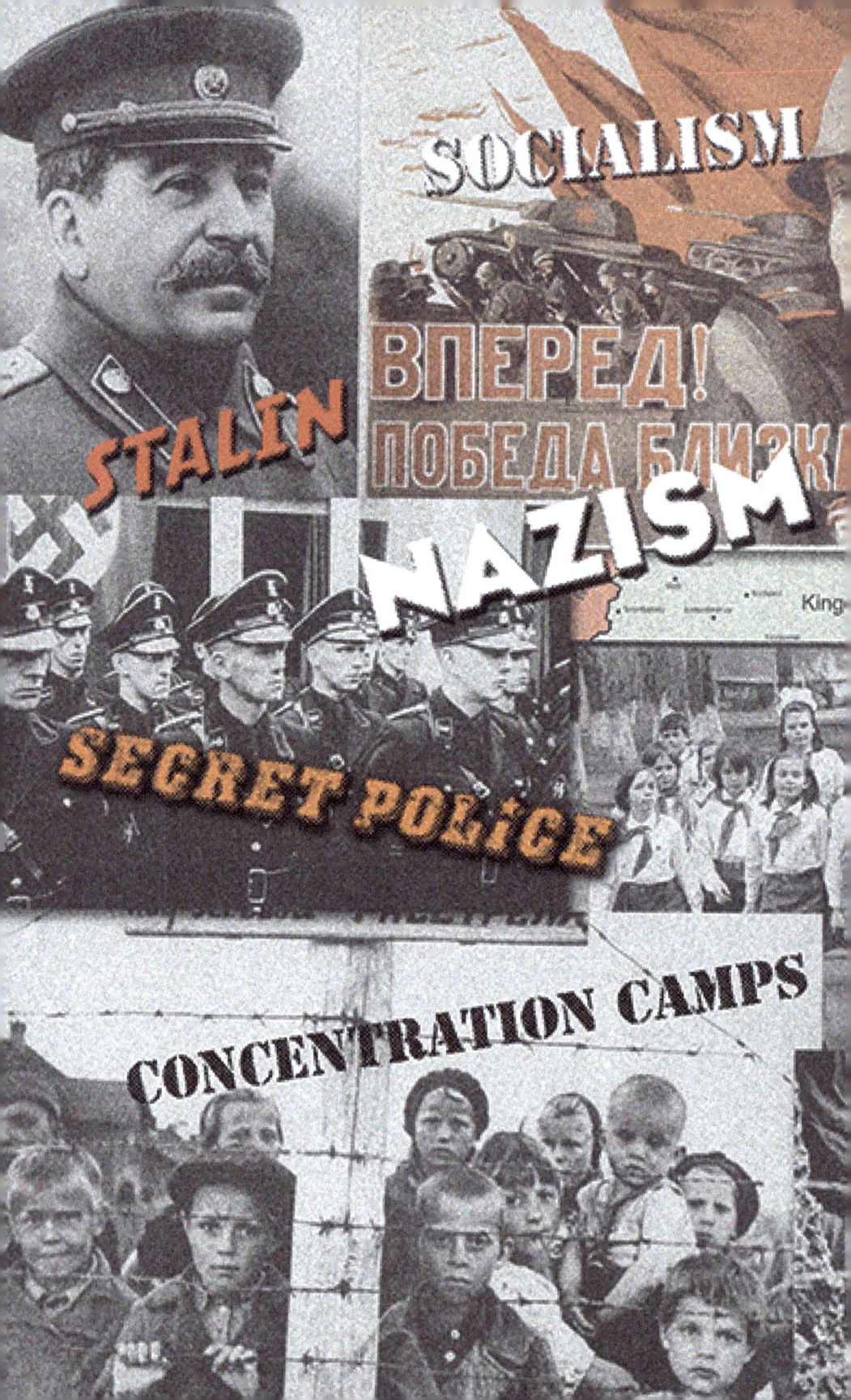

DESTINATION FREEDOM

Escape from Tyranny

By Susanne M. Reyto

DESTINATION FREEDOM

www.destinationfreedom.net

Copyright © 2020
by Susanne M. Reyto

All rights reserved.
It is not legal to reproduce, duplicate, or transmit any part of this document in either electronic means or printed format. Recording of this publication is strictly prohibited.

ISBN – 978-0-944581-02-5
eISBN 978-0-944581-03-2
Library of Congress Control Number: 2020918166

Published by:

Jet Publishing
Los Angeles, Ca

www.jetpublishing.com ~ books@jetpublishing.com

Acknowledgments:

This book is dedicated to my late parents, who have been my lifelong inspiration and would be very proud. Also, to my husband Robert and our family, whose constant support inspired me to write this book and to never stop teaching our future generations about our history and its significance for their future.

You taught me the meaning of love, Survival and the power of positive thinking.

Son-in-law Steve, daughter Michelle, granddaughter Nicole, husband Robert, and me.

Table of Contents

Prologue		P. 1
Chapter 1	Kyle's Classroom	P. 9
Chapter 2	Mother and Me	P. 20
Chapter 3	Schutzpass – Protective Passport	P. 26
Chapter 4	Life in the Ghetto	P. 31
Chapter 5	My Father	P. 34
Chapter 6	Liberation	P. 43
Chapter 7	After the War – Idyllic Years	P. 47
Chapter 8	Political Changes	P. 62
Chapter 9	Communism and Brainwashing	P. 68
Chapter 10	Escape from Hungary	P. 82
Chapter 11	Capture and Abduction	P. 86
Chapter 12	Prison Nursery	P. 92
Chapter 13	Imprisonment	P. 96
Chapter 14	Reunited	P. 103
Chapter 15	Life After Prison	P. 114
Chapter 16	Communist Deportation	P. 115
Chapter 17	Life in the Country	P. 121
Chapter 18	Remote Farm	P. 134
Chapter 19	Return from Captivity	P. 141
Chapter 20	Revolution	P. 148
Chapter 21	Attempted Escapes	P. 152
Chapter 22	Leaving Hungary	P. 157
Chapter 23	Vienna	P. 161
Chapter 24	Leaving for Australia	P. 167
Chapter 25	Life in Australia	P. 171
Chapter 26	Leaving Australia	P. 179
Chapter 27	Arriving in Los Angeles and Leaving	P. 182
Epilogue		P. 188

"Thank the past for all the lessons it taught you; anticipate the future for all the blessings it has in store for you."
quote by: Matshona Dhliwayo

Central/Eastern Europe after the fall of Communism

Prologue

Over seventy-five years have passed since the final days of World War II, when, it is commonly believed, the wartime suffering in Europe came to an end. However, that is not the case; the same dark history responsible for 85 million deaths (3 percent of the 1940 world population) continues to play out in various parts of the world.

My life's mission is to educate and inform the next generations so that my personal history does not recur, now or in the future. To be more accurately aware of the difference between truth and fiction, it is imperative to tune into as many versions of "the facts" as possible and from as many diverse views as are available. Knowledge is power. Listen and learn from others, and then draw your own conclusions.

Kyle, my grandson, is a history lover, so he and I have often discussed what is going on in the world and how these issues relate to my years growing up in Hungary. In some countries today, many parallels exist between their current political climate and philosophy and those of Nazi and Communist Europe. I am concerned about the knowledge and depth of Kyle's awareness and the revised versions of history young Americans are learning in school today.

Kyle often asked me about how I grew up in Hungary. When I related to him that my childhood was filled with Nazi persecution, imprisonment, and kidnapping, and that later my parents and I were forced to live in an internment camp and endure daily psychological torment at the hands of the Communist regime, he became eager to learn more about my firsthand experiences. His questions soon evolved into stories about my family's struggle to survive — first under the rule of the tyrannical Nazis and then under the similarly barbaric Communist regime — and also our attempts to escape our occupied homeland. I often told him about our unstoppable dream of living our future in freedom and, how, through sheer will and courage, we eventually made that dream a reality

Kyle was particularly interested in hearing about my life because his English class had just finished studying Anne Frank's diary. "That's great, Kyle," I said. "I'm glad your class will know about the evils of the Nazi era, but I hope your teacher will also tell you about the secrecy, misinformation, lies, terror, and deception of the following regime to rule Hungary — the precursor to Communism. Although we survived the Nazis only to experience the horrors of Communism, we didn't know why we were being maltreated. We only became aware of the details in 1989, after the fall of Communism, when documents finally surfaced."

"How did you find out?" Kyle asked.

"Purely by chance. At that time, we didn't have iPhones or Google. During a trip to Budapest in May 2002, your grandfather Robert and I had an amazing, unexpected experience."

"Tell me about it."

"The most dreaded address in Budapest during the Nazi occupation was Andrássy Street 60. It was an architecturally beautiful building that was used by the Nazis during World War II to interrogate, torture, or kill their suspects. Unfortunately, the interrogations continued in the same manner under the Communist regime. The building has since been converted into a museum, aptly called HOUSE OF TERROR.

"While we lived in Hungary, we knew that most people taken to that dreaded address seldom left alive. Visiting the museum, we had the opportunity to see, read, and hear the stories for ourselves. It was a truly memorable experience: people whispering and some wiping tears from their eyes while reading documents and viewing photographs. Visiting the cells in the basement where the torture and hangings took place made the horrors come alive. One of the floors was dedicated entirely to Communism. 'Susanne, come quickly. Look at this!' Robert yelled, suddenly. My heart raced and, for a moment, my legs wouldn't move. 'These are actual documents of your deportation,' he said as he pointed to the walls that had copies of documents and newspaper articles plastered onto it. 'This is amazing! We must get copies. These represent stories of your life.'

Newspaper article describing story of displacement

"I was stunned. Two walls are completely wallpapered with copies of official documents and newspaper clippings describing my family's suffering. They served as the blueprint for the execution of the Communist prescription for horror. As my eyes scanned the walls covered with images, I felt myself drowning in emotions. I didn't know where to look first. Every document seemed important, exposing one of the darkest periods in Hungary's history — like an instant replay of my life.

"You know, Kyle, it is inconceivable that I had to wait fifty-five years to learn these facts about my own life, but I am grateful that it is now available for all to see. I was determined to get copies of the documents, knowing they would mean a lot to my mother.

"Were you able to get them?" he asked with curiosity.

"Yes, but getting them was almost a miracle. We went through a lot of red tape and security checks just to enter the Hungarian archives. When we finally reached the right department, we had to twist arms and sweet-talk the staff into providing them for us. Forty-five minutes later, when they finally located the file, one of the women explained that this formerly large dossier was originally the prime minister's personal file, but that it now consisted of only 115 pages — a scant reminder of that turbulent era. Many of the papers disappeared or were burned during the Communist uprising in 1956 and in its fall in 1989."

"It's unreal," Kyle said, shaking his head. "It's really cool to find part of your personal history displayed in a museum. I wish you would come to my class and talk about it."

I smiled. I was touched.

"It would be my greatest pleasure, Kyle! Ask your teacher if she would allow it, and I'll be there whenever you can arrange it."

It seemed I had opened a small window for him to look into the past. A past that was not just a textbook filled with statements and dates, but a past he could see, feel, and relate to.

As he was walking away, he smiled and said, "I will talk to my teacher and arrange for you to come. But remember, we need to continue this later. I want to hear more. I want to hear everything."

I thought about standing in front of his class and making a meaningful presentation to youngsters who might not have much knowledge of history and even less information about the Holocaust. I realized that, over the years, I had rarely discussed my childhood experiences with my parents, as they wanted to protect me from previous "hurts" and unpleasant memories. While some things I remember clearly, I would need to ask Mother to fill in many important details about my birth and the couple of years that followed. I was worried because I wasn't sure how she would respond. Would she be willing to reopen closed wounds? Would she be angry at me for asking? I thought a lot about how to approach her, but time was of the essence.

I started by telling her about Kyle's invitation and asked her to help me with some facts. I was amazed at her positive reaction. Mother was an astute, quick-thinking eighty-three-year-old, who, regardless of the unpleasant memories it dredged up, felt strongly about the importance of telling young people how we managed to live and survive under two brutal regimes. She immediately started telling stories and recalling images she had stored in her memory for over fifty years. I had to grab paper and pen to make notes.

Mother's hope was that the children of Kyle's generation realize how fortunate they are to grow up in the land of freedom — the United States of America.

Mother and Me

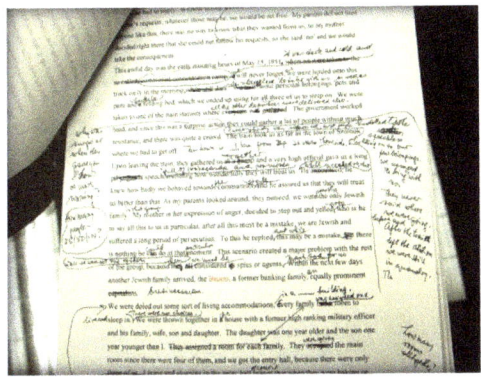 

The Manuscript　　　　　　　　　　　Mother sitting by the computer

To make it easier for her and to ensure that we had all the facts we needed, we gave her a tape recorder, which, despite being technologically challenged, she learned to operate. When she finished her story, she and I sat at the computer to transcribe it. Together we checked dates and details, making sure that we had a historically accurate account.

My husband, Robert, was also born in Hungary and, because he was a university student in 1956, he was exposed to a radical political perspective — the outspoken viewpoint of fellow students that helped instigate the Hungarian uprising of 1956. Whenever I would mention certain events of my background to him, and, despite the fact that we were living in the same city of Budapest at the same time, they came as a revelation to him. Because of the hostile environment and the secretive way we had to live — not trusting anyone, even family members — he had no real knowledge of how many Hungarians, like us, were suffering at that time. We often listened to each other in shock and disbelief.

Living in Los Angeles with six- to ten-lane freeways reminds me of how different it was riding on a bumpy country road in Hungary in December 1949, the time my family tried to escape their homeland — first soiled by the

Nazi reign of terror, and followed by the desperate life forced upon us by Communism. We had been only thirty minutes from freedom and yet could not reach our destination. It would be another eight dismal years before we had the good fortune to make our escape to the West.

Chapter 1
KYLE'S CLASSROOM

I arrived at Kyle's school by 9 a.m. and was both thrilled and surprised when he asked if I would be willing to speak not only to his class, but to all six of Ms. Anderson's classes. Ms. Anderson was lovely and understood the importance of having the topic taught by a survivor. I hoped to give them enough information to expose them effectively to that period of history, but I was concerned about how the youngsters would receive me and how I could make the day meaningful for them. What would make the greatest impact on these fourteen-year-old students? I wanted them to know that they were only a year older than I was when I left Hungary with my family and that that was the turning point in my life and the start of my long and perilous journey to freedom.

The first class I spoke to was quiet and listened attentively. Since they had not had any previous lessons on the Holocaust, Ms. Anderson helped out when the students became confused. Her comments helped me with the next classes, too, where I incorporated more specifics for a clearer understanding.

Another of my concerns that day was that my thirty-six-year-old daughter had never heard about my early life, and she would be exposed to it for the first time. I wondered how she would react and how it would affect her, particularly since she would be hearing it repeatedly all day.

Ms. Anderson (on the right) and me

Kyle

"Boys and girls, this is Kyle's grandmother, Mrs. Reyto," Ms. Anderson said to the class. "You are fortunate to have someone like her to share her firsthand experiences, not only of her life during the Nazi occupation, but also under Communism." The students sat at their desks, Kyle in the front row to my right side, and I stood in front of them with the blackboard behind me.

As I looked around, I noticed each child appeared interested and focused on me. Not one person spoke or fidgeted. My worries disappeared.

I said, "I am very glad and honored to be here to speak to you today. I would like to introduce you to my husband, Robert, standing in the back, and our daughter, Michelle — Kyle's mom. I hope you will find my story meaningful. Please feel free to interrupt if you have any questions.

"I was born on March 19, 1944, just six days before the Germans invaded and occupied Hungary. Has anyone heard of or traveled to Hungary?" Several hands went up. "Even if you have never been there, at least some of you have heard about it. To make it easier to understand the history of Germany's spread of power, I have placed the map of Europe on the blackboard, showing Hungary's strategic location. I was a baby during the occupation, so the early part of my story comes to me through my mother's recollections.

"You may have heard other people relating their experiences through books, film, or personal remembrances. Everybody has a story worth telling, and worth learning from.

"After the Nazi invasion we lived under very difficult conditions in Budapest. The Nazis wanted to get rid of us Jews, but thanks to two wonderful humanitarian diplomats, our lives were spared. Carl Lutz from Switzerland and Raoul Wallenberg from Sweden distributed protective documents called Schutzpasses, designating us as citizens of their respective countries. By honoring those so-called official documents, which classified us as foreign nationals, the Nazis had no right to arrest, relocate, or harm us. While there were about 10,000 of these original documents, an underground Jewish youth group reproduced perfect additional copies, putting an approximate total of about 100,000 in circulation. Thanks to these permits, 100,000 Jews of Budapest were given a chance to survive. But, while they shielded us and those others fortunate enough to get them, their protection was temporary. During this period, Jews also enjoyed protection in certain safe houses, which were marked with the yellow star. So, please be aware that while so much of the population was engaged in malicious activities, there were also decent, caring individuals, who often risked their own lives to save ours."

They, and others like them, were called Righteous Gentiles. These Righteous Among Nations, commemorated for their courage and compassion, are now honored at a memorial park in Israel, called the Garden of the Righteous in Jerusalem. These caring and courageous people represent that portion of the world population who, in any generation, can be counted upon to help those in need.

"While the *Schutzpass* gave us some measure of security for a few months, we were forced to live mostly underground under deplorable conditions with cold, wet cement floors designated for wood storage — not living quarters. Conditions deteriorated even further, and took a major turning point one day. In October 1044, my mother, her two sisters, and their mother (my grandmother), together with the majority of the remaining Jews in Budapest were marched at gunpoint to a soccer field where the Hungarian Nazis sorted people into groups before shipping them to concentration camps. Despite her pleas, my mom was forced to leave me behind with two elderly ladies. Assembled in the field, the women were forbidden to talk to one another.

"Then, something wonderful happened. A man in Nazi uniform came up to my mother and pushed her out of the crowd, all the way to the gate. Once she was outside, he left her and disappeared.

"Mother had been given a split-second chance to come back to me, while her less fortunate mother and sisters were shipped to a concentration camp. She ran toward our apartment, and almost collapsed upon arrival. She found me screaming, but thankful she was back.

"As I looked around the classroom, I kept watching for Kyle's reactions. As he put his hands over his eyes, I wondered what he was thinking. Ms. Anderson had warned me that some of the boys were talkative, but she hoped that they would be respectful and listen. I felt they were attentive and were with me and my story, which I could see was affecting them all. One boy, who had been doodling at first, put down his pen and listened. There was such quietness in the room; it seemed everyone was touched.

I continued, "When those fake documents were no longer honored, some people were taken away to die, or, like us, were forced to move into the ghetto — which was, more or less, a geographical area where people of similar background, ethnicity, and/or religion lived. The Jewish ghetto in Budapest covered a large area of several square blocks. The Nazis had built a wall around it, locked the gates, and guarded it with uniformed gun-toting soldiers.

We were allowed outside the walls for only two hours in the morning and two hours in the afternoon. Food was scarce and much of the time we were near starvation. We lived in the ghetto for about six weeks during the freezing December winter of 1944. Much of the time, deprived of warm clothing, we spent down in the unheated bomb shelters with their cement floors. Thankfully, six weeks later, the Russian Army arrived in Hungary and defeated the Germans. Liberating Budapest and the rest of the country took weeks because the Germans didn't surrender easily.

"We were thankful to the Soviet Union for defeating Germany in 1945, but our gratitude ended when we realized they planned to stay on and impose Communist rule over our country. Not everybody trusted them, and it took the Communists three years before they won an election. During that three-year period my parents were slowly able to re-establish our comfortable lifestyle.

"Under Communism we were never told the truth; we heard only government-controlled misinformation — propaganda. The news was always suppressed; everything was a secret. We were afraid to discuss events with others because we couldn't trust anyone. People were taken away under false accusation or without explanation. Children were brainwashed or lied to in school. They were encouraged to report on their family members, even parents, if they heard things at home that sounded contrary to what they were told at their schools' brainwashing sessions.

"Life deteriorated and became difficult. My parents wanted to leave Hungary, but when we tried to escape, the border patrol captured us and imprisoned us. I was five years old when my father was sentenced to one year in prison and my mother to eight months. Right after the sentencing, a female guard kidnapped me from my parents and took me to a prison nursery, an orphanage, where I joined children whose parents had been caught before us. For quite a while I didn't know what had happened to my parents. Added to the fear and unpleasant surroundings, the food, geared toward the appetite of country folk, was awful — both to look at and to taste. Instead of keeping us healthy as they had promised, they would inject us with various illnesses and use us for medical experiments. I was lucky that I only developed chicken pox, because a five-year-old cousin of mine was given polio. Her family had tried to escape sometime before us, but the conditions were not as strict back then, and, unlike us, they were released after a few days.

"About a week after becoming infected she became very ill, developed a fever accompanied by muscle aches, and began throwing up. The following day, the muscle pain grew stronger, and she became paralyzed. Only after the paralysis set in did they diagnose her with polio. Fortunately, she had a mild case and did not require confinement to an 'iron lung' — a machine designed to help polio victims breathe. With her mother's help she began extensive therapy to mobilize her limbs, and after a few weeks she regained limited mobility. Due to her parents' ongoing dedication, she has been able to live a normal life, except for her dependency on two crutches.

"After I recuperated, a friend of my parents came to get me from the orphanage and took me to an aunt and uncle where I stayed until my parents' release. After about a year, we were together again.

"By now it was the end of 1950, and owning a business was no longer permitted. The government took over every private enterprise, and former owners became employees of their own companies. Everyone would now work for the government in what were called collectives.

"We had a beautiful home, but, according to the government, it was too fancy and we did not deserve it. The regime mandated that regular citizens had less while their leaders had considerably more. When many of these new leaders came to live in the city, Budapest experienced a shortage of apartments. To make more living space available, they devised a plan to displace people like us — to move us to the country and bring the country folks into the city. This order was called the Communist Deportation.

"There was practically no public outcry because when people found out about it, they were too afraid to criticize the regime or even to discuss it. Anyone who spoke out was called a dissident and many were punished severely, with long prison terms. We never knew how many other people were affected, where they were, or how long this decree would be enforced. Everything was classified as secret. We only discovered the facts fifty years later, after seeing those declassified documents in the House of Terror Museum.

"How would you feel if suddenly you were faced with the total disruption of your lives, separation from family and friends, loss of personal property, and even death threats?

"I hope some of my experiences will make you realize how lucky you are to be an American and that you must never take your freedom for granted. That is a precious commodity we did not have during Nazism or the Communist regime that followed.

"As different as they were, they were variations of the same: injustice, prejudice, subjugation, and loss of freedoms for which we in the U.S. are protected by our Constitution. As you can see, religious intolerance and bigotry was a way of life then, which, 70 years later, we are still experiencing. Learning this vital lesson at your age should make it easier to face and defeat in the future, should such injustices come your way.

"By the time I was thirteen, almost the age you are now, we were finally allowed to leave Hungary, but, at the last security checkpoint, we had a major problem with one of my favorite possessions — a miniature tea set, which I consider my lucky charm. Since I hadn't realized it should have been declared to the authorities, they assumed I was trying to smuggle it out of the country. Instinctively, I told them it was one of my toys, which was a white lie that probably saved us from deportation or worse. Over the years, that harrowing experience has made my tea set all the more meaningful to me. It sits in a special place in our house, a china cabinet in our living room, where I look at it almost every day. Seeing it symbolizes optimism for me and fills me with joy and gratitude. I wonder if you have a special something that reminds you of your earlier years and manages to evoke a smile.

Miniature tea set. The tray that holds the pieces is only about 3" by 4 ½".

"I have lived through Nazism and Communism and I hope there will never be another fanatic group to come along and control our lives. Soviet-style Communism is behind us, but other styles of Communism still exist in China, North Korea, Cuba, and Venezuela, where they wield total political control over their people. How do you feel about Communist Cuba being located only ninety miles off the coast of Florida?

"Given the right circumstances, Communism could once again rear its ugly head. I hope that after today's presentation, knowing what my family and

I went through, you will be better prepared and motivated to stand up against tyranny in any form it takes. Having learned so much over the years from personal hardships, I came to realize that in all bad things there is also something good. A strong formal education and parental insights have heightened my awareness and my ability to cope with adversity.

"When you travel you come to realize how other people live, and you become familiar with the value systems of other cultures. What our lifestyle offers may not apply as well to other countries, considering their standard of living and their politics. But, once you have experienced their culture and their environment, you will be in a better position to evaluate their worldview Not everyone can live as we do in the U.S., nor, in some cases, would they want to.

"The internet has brought people and countries closer together than ever before. Instead of waiting weeks for news, we have instant access from anywhere in the world, 24/7. Following the horrific events of September 11th, 2001, we have learned to think differently and are less likely to take our freedoms for granted. I cannot help but compare my early struggles under tyranny with how the terrorists and anarchists of today are attempting to destroy our civilized world. These fanatical groups are committed to abolishing artifacts and ideas that are foreign, even hostile, to their ways, but are so fundamental to our own. These radicals reject our form of democracy, as their worldview forbids freedom of any opinion that conflicts with theirs. That is why you must learn, study, and be well informed — to ensure your individual rights and to preserve and protect your beliefs and your way of life. Try to recognize right from wrong. But always respect others for their similarities as well as their differences.

"Our U.S. Constitution and our freedom of speech are the foundation upon which America was established and upon which it builds toward its future.

"Later on, I will describe how my family lived a secretive life, unable to share anything, even with our close relatives. Can you imagine not being free to express yourself for fear of your life? In totalitarian countries, such is the norm. You may not speak freely, as it may be used against you and considered treasonous. Would you be able to live that way? Unfortunately, people living under such dictatorships have no choice but to tolerate the system. Some who have been living under such regimes all or most of their lives don't even have a basis for comparison.

"Nobody believed the Nazis came to hurt them, which is why millions were caught off guard, and were killed. Terrorists believe that their way is the only way, and they will falsify information repeatedly with the goal of making you believe them. Strive always to learn the truth, knowing it may be buried under layers of lies and distortions.

"It is my sincere desire to inspire you with my family's tenacious journey from oppression to freedom, and to show you my deep appreciation for this country I now call my own: The United States of America.

"And, finally, no matter what, have hope and faith. There is always another tomorrow. Evil will eventually be defeated by the power of the righteous. Treasure our U.S. Constitution; it's there to protect you. I hope my experiences will help to instill in you the importance of education, awareness, and tolerance for others. Never take your rights for granted and don't let others get away with lies to serve their political gain. Take responsibility!"

Chapter 2

MOTHER AND ME

My mother faced the Nazi occupation with courage and grace. Her views of what happened during that period and into the years of Communism that followed help to enrich my story and bring it alive.

<u>My mother's story:</u>
In 1942, your father was called in for the compulsory Hungarian military service. At that time, he was the supplier of firefighting equipment to the government, and they used his expertise to their benefit. In exchange, he received government protection. Assigned to work in the central distribution warehouse, he was given special privileges not granted to other men, such as wearing civilian clothes and occasional visits home. During one of his visits in early 1944, anticipating his absence at the time of your birth, he withdrew a large sum of money from the bank and left it with me for expenses. Nobody knew what the future held, but we sensed the coming of political upheaval and even more severe food shortages. News traveled slowly, but the rumblings about anti-Jewish treatment in Austria filtered into Hungary. Your father's foresight of a deteriorating Hungary proved accurate.

Left alone without any assistance during the last few weeks of my pregnancy, I felt frightened and insecure, and I was forced to move in with my parents.

It was Monday, March 13, 1944. My father and two sisters took me to the hospital. A milestone in Dad's and my life that he was not able to share with me. He was allowed to come home for one day, but only a few days after your birth.

My doctor was a researcher and a kind human being, and he knew our circumstances. He also knew we were Jewish, and that your father was away. So he wanted to help. Despite the political climate, as a Christian, he treated me with great concern and compassion. He was aware of the goings-on, especially because his small research institute was located in the inner courtyard of the facility, which was Budapest's main government hospital.

In those days, new mothers were kept in the hospital for seven to ten days after delivery, so I was scheduled to be released on Monday, the 20th of March.

While still in the hospital, my parents called every morning to inquire about the previous night and our new baby. Strangely, the day before my expected release, I did not hear from them, but concluded that there had to be a good reason. My concern grew when I noticed the nurses hadn't come into my room that morning, as was their routine. A lot of commotion in the corridor signaled me that something was wrong. Then, later, things became more frantic, and one of the nurses told me that early that morning Germany had invaded Hungary, and established their headquarters on the hospital grounds. It was March 19, 1944 — and there I was with a six-day-old baby.

Now I was justifiably worried about my release from the hospital — knowing that anti-Semitic forces had filled the streets, and gun-toting enemy soldiers were marching through the city. My fear intensified as the time of my release grew near. Then, like an angel, my doctor flew into my room and said, "I have ordered an ambulance to take you home, and arranged for a sign, 'Infectious Disease,' to be placed on the sides of the ambulance. Hopefully, this would keep people away from the ambulance and we could get you home." He also instructed me to have someone other than a family member accompany me, someone who was not Jewish.

Following his advice, I asked one of our employees to ride home with us. Due to the frightening sign on the car, nobody bothered us. I was grateful to my doctor for our safe drive to your grandparents.

Budapest is divided by the Danube River into Buda, which is hilly, and Pest, which is flat. On the Buda side were mainly single-family houses, whereas on the Pest side people lived in apartment buildings, where the heating materials for each unit were stored in large basements. When needed, supplies had to be carried upstairs. As the war was brewing, supplies were diminishing, and the basement storage areas were converted into bomb shelters. Since the space was originally used for storage, it had bare walls, cement floors, no windows or ventilation, poor lighting, and no heating. Prior to the Nazi invasion, when the political atmosphere was merely turbulent, and not yet the blazing inferno it was to become, people made it more bearable by putting in additional lights and benches. Communication in those days was problematic. With no television and only limited radio, the population tried to prepare for the uncertain times ahead, but could not imagine the dire circumstances facing them.

When the war reached Hungary in full force, everybody suffered. But the Jews suffered the most. When the Germans invaded in March 1944, Miklos Horthy was the Hungarian leader. When he tried to disengage from Nazi Germany, he was deposed and, in October, the Hungarian anti-Semitic fascist militia, the Arrow Cross Party, took over. Given free rein to increase the violence and control over the Jews, the regime's leader, Imre Szalasi, constantly issued new discrimination laws, making their living conditions increasingly unbearable. After the Russians liberated Budapest in January 1945, Szalasi was caught and hung publicly, to the satisfaction of many.

Jews were once again the object of discrimination, and, for identification, we had to wear a yellow star at all times. The size, color, and placement of the star were specifically defined: a 10x10cm (about 4" by 4") canary yellow, six-

pointed star, which had to be worn directly above the heart. Whenever I took you for a stroll in the afternoon, not only did I have to wear a yellow star, but I also had to place one on the stroller.

In Hungary it was the simple star, but in other countries, in the center, it said "Jew" in whatever their native language was. Whereas elsewhere, the star was only "expected" to be worn, in Hungary the law was strictly enforced. Hungary was the last of the countries to be occupied and, by then, the Germans had become more rigid and strict.

Jewish children had to wear the star, as well. Credit: Yad Vashem

A large, six-pointed yellow star marked the front door of all designated Jewish apartment buildings, where whole families lived in one room.

Fortunately, my parents already lived in one of these buildings, so we were able to remain there. However, many other people were forced to move in with us. Each room in the apartment became home to a different family and everyone had to share the single kitchen and bathroom. Living in such close quarters put everyone in a fragile mental state. As it became almost impossible to get food, the situation grew worse. Mothers had no milk to feed their children, and babies — you, included — cried constantly from hunger. Hunger, worry, and exhaustion frazzled everyone's nerves. Fear pervaded every moment of every day.

Chapter 3

"SCHUTZPASS" – PROTECTIVE PASSPORT

Mother was eager to tell me everything — the bad as well as the good. She always spoke with gratitude about the two humanitarians who worked hard and creatively to save Jews. Thanks to them, we are alive.

During the Nazi reign of terror, many Jews in several countries were mercilessly put to death. Before World War II, there had been approximately 800,000 Jews throughout Hungary, and only those living in Budapest were protected by the Schutzpass.

Adolph Eichmann, who was in charge of the Nazi labor force, came to Hungary in early May 1944 to gather the Jews for transport to their factories. The Nazis conducted major businesses and manufactured ammunition and building materials, including bricks. Between May and July, in a six-week period, 600,000 people were transported — the majority of them to Auschwitz. Before being taken, they were sorted, divided into two groups — one for the healthy who were able to work and the other for the older, sickly, and children, who, immediately after arrival at the camps, were marched to their deaths. Ultimately, by the time the war ended, a majority had died — some due to living conditions, starvation, or hard labor, and others, who had become too weak to work, were killed. Sadly, many of those who survived ended up dying on their difficult journey home.

According to estimates in 2000, there were between 80,000 and 100,000 Jews left in Hungary. Hungarian Jews can thank at least two God-sent diplomats for helping us survive the Nazi slaughter.

Raoul Wallenberg, the Swedish diplomat, and Carl Lutz, the Swiss Consul, both performed incredibly heroic acts. Carl Lutz, especially, risked his own life to save others. Both men became world-renowned for their humanitarian efforts during those years of hate and evil. The lesser-known Carl Lutz acted on his own, without his country's orders or consent. Raoul Wallenberg was specifically on orders by the Swedish Foreign Ministry to help Hungary's Jews.

From 1942 to 1945, Lutz was in charge of the foreign interest section in the Swiss Embassy in Budapest, representing many countries, including the U.S. and United Kingdom, which were at war with Hungary. Lutz took a personal interest in helping the persecuted Jews. One of his first steps was to recognize those persons as American Citizens, who could produce letters from American friends or relatives, confirming their efforts to get them into the U.S. Then, starting in May 1944, Lutz provided documents to other people who held any type of foreign papers, certifying them as part of a Swiss collective passport for immigration purposes. These documents, which created the impression that their holders were Swiss nationals, formed the basis for the "safe conduct passport" — the Schutzpass — which Lutz and Wallenberg later issued to a good number of Jews.

Lutz first issued 7,800 documents, the Hungarian government limit, but in reality, he distributed many times that number. These documents identified their owners as citizens of Switzerland, and thus theoretically immunized them from Hungarian laws. He also provided thousands of additional blank documents together with original stamps and signatures to a young underground Zionist group, whose members forged and distributed thousands more to helpless Jews. These forgeries were perfect and could pass for the real thing. Lutz also established safe houses in Budapest, and, with his wife, Gertrud, rescued Jews from being shipped to concentration camps, deportation centers, and death marches.

Raoul Wallenberg was secretary of the Swedish Consulate in Budapest from July 1944 to 1945. In addition to issuing tens of thousands of Schutzpasses, he also organized the collection and dissemination of food, medicine, and medical assistance. Wallenberg also saved thousands of lives, including ours and members of my immediate family. We often wonder what would have happened to us without their intervention.

So many documents were issued that the Nazi plans for deportation became boggled and confusing. The Schutzpasses — both real and forged — had no actual value according to international law, yet for a precious time they saved many lives. We can never be thankful enough to Wallenberg and Lutz for their unselfish bravery.

We were fortunate to have both the Swedish and Swiss papers because my brother worked at both offices as a young gofer. It was helpful to have more than one, because sometimes the Nazis took one and tore it up in anger.

The Schutzpass granted us some security. When the Nazis detained us, they allowed us to remain in our building, or directed us to another "protected house." While moving from house to house kept us alive, the living conditions became more unbearable. We had little to eat, and we were often sick. With twenty-five to thirty people jammed into each small room, sleep was out of the question. There were not enough beds or even enough room for everybody. We all had to lie on the cold, cement floor at night, pushed against other bodies, close enough to hear them breathing. No wonder, we suffered continually from bouts of pneumonia. Under those conditions, there was no chance to stay well or even to get better.

At that time, you were four months old, and we were only allowed to go outside from nine to eleven in the morning and two to four in the afternoon.

Anyone caught on the streets at any other time was captured, and either sent to a concentration camp or executed on the spot.

During those four hours, we had to shop for food, which was difficult. We not only had to go to different shops for each type of food, but everything was in short supply. Since there were no supermarkets, everything was sold in a specific store, like baked goods in a bakery, milk products in a dairy store, meat items in a butcher shop, etc. We had to stand in long lines to purchase whatever was available. Sometimes we would wait for hours, just for bread — only to reach the front of the line and learn there was none left.

Those who did venture out to get supplies often returned empty-handed, having been rejected either because of their Jewish yellow star or because of real food shortages. As hungry as we were, we were often afraid to go outside because of the frequent air raids and heavy bombings.

Non-Jews, on the other hand, did not have to stand in line. They were first to get served, so food seldom ran out for them. We tried to resolve our food needs by paying a non-Jewish neighbor to shop for us. Because it helped them financially, there were many people willing to assist us. Fortunately, I still had some of the money your father had left with me, so I was able to get the bare essentials. I was glad to pay the neighbors for their help and was grateful for their efforts. Without them, we might have starved.

By the middle of 1944, living in the protected houses while looking after a baby was extremely difficult. By this time, the Allied Forces were conducting daily bombings. The moment the siren sounded, we had to rush down to the shelters below. People were so concerned for their own lives, they paid no attention to anyone else, especially you and me, since we were not regular residents of the building. I had to quickly wrap you in a blanket, put you in a basket, and carry you down to the basement shelter with the help of a neighbor, all the while fighting a stampede of people.

The siren alerts during bathing were even more disturbing. I had to dress you in a hurry, grab necessities, and run. We never knew how long we would have to stay down there, or even what the next moment would bring.

For over four months, from July until the opening of the ghetto at the end of November, we were ordered from one protected house to another, always hoping the next building would be better. Yet, with every move, there was more misery, fewer people we knew, less food, less shelter, less space, and fewer basic living necessities.

After a while, even the buildings designated as safe no longer offered safety. The Hungarian Nazis, the uniformed Arrow Cross, ignored all the "official" papers, invaded houses at will, and gathered up whomever they wished in front of the building. Those who were young and in good physical condition were marched off to concentration camps for slave labor. Others were taken to the banks of the Danube River, executed, and pushed into the freezing water. This reality hit us hardest when it happened to some residents of our building.

Hungarian Nazis occupied several large apartment complexes. The upstairs was used for offices, and the basements served for torture and execution.

As conditions grew worse, survival was a matter of tenacity, sheer willpower, and good health. Above all, it was thanks to the selfless acts of a few compassionate, courageous people.

Chapter 4

LIFE IN THE GHETTO

The Hungarian-supported Nazi Party established the Arrow Cross military units, which enforced their laws viciously, searched for young, able-bodied Jews, and disregarded all prior documents that provided the so-called foreign protection. To make sure everyone obeyed, they terrorized Jews wherever they could, with impunity.

Nazi Swastika

Arrow Cross Party Symbol

By the end of November 1944, the Nazis had raided the Swiss- and Swedish-protected houses. They gathered those who were left, mostly women and children, and forced them out onto the streets, and eventually into the ghetto of Budapest, which opened on November 29.

According to historical records from the Hungarian Jewish Archives, by then there were 63,000 people in the ghetto, which covered many square blocks in the middle of the city and had four entrances surrounding the large Dohány

Synagogue. So many people were crammed into those apartments that family members residing in one part of the ghetto didn't know the whereabouts of other members of the family for the entire duration of their imprisonment there. At first, only certain streets and buildings were designated, but later they built a wall with solid iron gates, closing off streets at the boundary lines. On December 10, 1944, the gates were locked from the outside, and police and military guards were posted to prevent anybody from escaping. We lived like this from November 29, 1944, to January 18, 1945, liberation day.

All we could think about was having enough food to eat and stay alive. Since I was often starving, I did not produce enough milk to feed you. It was so cold that I never knew whether you were crying from the cold, the hunger, or both. I felt helpless and powerless to make you feel better, so I held you in my arms all the time, trying to relieve some of your pain and discomfort. Often your crying disturbed other people around us, who were also cold and hungry. While bombs were falling, nerves were frayed, and people were extremely sensitive. The last thing they wanted to hear was a screaming baby, reminding them of their own misery.

Food became even more difficult to get than before. In some of the ghetto buildings there were original residents with food stored in their apartments. Some of these people were willing to cook and provide food for others in exchange for money or valuables.

A central kitchen, located away from the ghetto at the Budapest Jewish Community Center, supplied a meager amount of food. As little as it was, it probably saved our lives. The bombings were so constant that the men who were sent for food were afraid to leave the shelters and many who did leave never came back. They were either killed in the bombings or captured by Nazi soldiers and sent to concentration camps.

When we first arrived at the ghetto, we were fortunate to find a bed to sleep in, up against a wall. On one particular night, you and I were in our room when a tremendous bomb hit the building next to ours, almost leveling it. It was a horrible experience; our whole building shook, and the noise, smoke, dust, and the screaming of frightened people overwhelmed us. The sound of falling bricks and broken glass was deafening. As you and I huddled on the bed, hugging each other, the wall beside us suddenly began to crumble; we watched as our "safety wall" came down around us. Our bed was left intact — we were fine, though shaken — but now we were sitting in the open air. The room was totally exposed to the outside. One wrong step, and we could have fallen from the third floor to the street below.

I remember vividly that terrifying moment — picking you up and carrying you away from all the smoke, debris, and freezing cold air. Now, where were we to go? The bomb shelter. Bombings were so frequent that we practically lived in the shelter, which had only bare walls and lacked facilities for washing or bathing. Since there was no heat, the water was often so cold that it froze. Sometimes weeks went by without our washing or bathing.

Yet, in every bad situation there were fleeting moments of great good. Our family physician lived in our building, and his wife went upstairs to their apartment to look for some medication for you. You were constantly crying, but after we got some of the medicine into you, you began to improve. Recovery was a slow process, but at least we kept you from getting worse. Barely recovered from one episode, though, you became ill with something else. During the first nine months of your life you were always sick. Constantly worried about your health, I kept praying and hoping for conditions to improve, or at the very least, for milder weather.

Down in the cellar, the awful days went by slowly, until suddenly, on the morning of January 16, 1945, rumors started to surface from people who had ventured outside the building. It seemed the Russian army was fighting nearby, and they were rapidly approaching. We prayed hard for their success. The next morning at dawn, a Russian soldier appeared at the ghetto gates and told us that we would be free within twenty-four hours.

Chapter 5

MY FATHER

My mother and I spent that whole period together. After all, she was nursing me. But, at the same time, my father experienced extreme hardship. His ability to remain optimistic gave him the strength to survive.

In 1993, my dad was eighty-six and in failing health. Despite being only five foot three, with his ever-present warmth and charisma, he commanded enormous attention whenever he entered a room.

I often heard my parents say they wished they had had another child, especially since Dad always wanted a son. But, due to circumstances, there was never a right time.

When my daughter, Michelle, married Steve, his son, Kyle, was six years old and lived with his mother but spent weekends with his father and Michelle. That arrangement gave my father an opportunity to develop a loving relationship with him. Dad's dreams of having a boy were answered when Kyle joined our family.

After Dad died, Kyle frequently asked Mother about him, After all, they were married fifty-three years, and she knew him best. The more I learned about him, the more questions I had.

My mother tells the story: *Your father and I were very different personalities. I admired his positive attitude, which was one of his greatest assets. I am so glad that much of that rubbed off on you. I remember him saying often, "The pessimist sees a problem in every opportunity, while the optimist sees an opportunity in every problem." He truly lived by that motto.*

After his basic schooling, in the late 1920s, he began to work in the family fire-fighting equipment business, and apprenticed with his uncle, Wilmos Biro, who received his engineering degree from a university in Germany at the turn of the century. Wilmos discovered that fires had "personalities," each type responding differently to various chemicals and methods of firefighting. At that time, firefighting was quite primitive; basically, it used only water. As a result of his findings, Wilmos invented portable fire extinguishers as we know them today. After completing his education in Germany, he returned to Hungary, where he introduced the new technology. Wilmos patented the various types of extinguishers, each one appropriate for a different type of fire. The dry chemical extinguisher, powder type, is the most common because it is effective on all types of fires. Carbon dioxide extinguishers are generally used in areas containing sensitive electrical equipment because carbon dioxide, a gas, leaves no residue and will not damage materials. Back then, these were revelations.

In 1935, your father started his own business, and it flourished. By the time war broke out in Europe in 1940, his company was a household name in Hungary. He had named it NOVARA after the famous ship of the Austro-Hungarian fleet, comparing his cutting-edge business with the legendary cutting-edge vessel.

Your dad became the supplier of fire extinguishers to the government and the military. His company equipped official buildings and public transportation vehicles, like buses, streetcars, and the underground railway. NOVARA's customers included the Hungarian Army and Navy, and numerous private companies like Shell Oil. With hard work he was able to build up the business and become acquainted with important officials, as well as military and police officers.

His equipment played an important, lifesaving role in the lives of the Hungarian people, and, once the war broke out, many government officials offered him assistance and protection. As long as the Hungarians remained in control, his security was assured. But once the Germans arrived, that protective status ended.

He wanted to continue his business during the war, but realized, as a Jew, it would be impossible. As always, however, he found a solution. He asked an old classmate and good friend from school in Mezotur, his hometown, to become a partner, because he was Christian. In early spring of 1944, he had the business listed in his friend's name, the only way his "Jewish" company could survive.

The business was saved and continued operation, but as the Nazis became more powerful, Dad became more vulnerable, personally, and was forced to go into hiding. By October 1944, conditions had worsened so much that he was dragged off to a forced labor camp, where the living conditions were horrific. The inmates were kept outdoors day and night and barely had enough to eat. Some of the men were infected with lice, and your father became ill with dysentery.

Taken to a small hospital for Jewish forced-labor servicemen, he was fortunate to find a soldier he knew from Budapest. The man had been a sportsman, who, during the early forties, had faced serious financial problems. Your father helped him financially through that difficult period so he could pursue his dreams. When he saw your father at the hospital, very sick and in need of assistance, he saw the opportunity to return the favor. He attended to him and cooked special food to treat the diarrhea and help him regain his strength.

As soon as your father was feeling well enough, the soldier helped him escape from the hospital, instructing him to hide at the town's train station and wait for a train leaving for Budapest. Father followed his advice. When the Budapest-bound train started to move, he jumped onboard and arrived in Budapest that night, the 23rd of October. The homecoming was short-lived. On October 28th, the Nazis captured him again, dragging him to the dreaded brick factory in Obuda, an old section of Budapest, which served as a gathering and sorting facility. From there thousands of men were forced to march daily toward the Austrian border, where trains were waiting to transport them to various concentration camps as either slave labor force, or to their last stop: the death camps.

Determined to survive, your father escaped once again and managed to return to Budapest. By now it was the end of November. Rifle-carrying Nazi hoodlums combed the streets, rounding up Jews. Your father was captured and thrown into a freight car with many others, then shipped like cattle to the Austrian border. When the train stopped at the border station, he escaped yet again. Because he was dressed as a villager — in shoes, shirt, and coat instead of boots and a thick pullover — he was able to run off, unnoticed. Whenever he returned to Budapest, he was sure to stay dressed that way to better blend in. Other men would have given up at this point — and many did. But each time he was captured, his will to live grew stronger.

When the train finally pulled away from the station, he began to walk the streets searching for a safe path back home. Along the way, he struck up a conversation with a chauffeur/driver awaiting his passenger — an important visiting official. Careful to watch every word he said, your dad gathered the guts to ask for a ride back to Budapest. Since he appeared to be a farmer, the driver had no problem with the request. Then, the passenger showed up — a Nazi officer in uniform. For a moment, your father panicked, and prayed that his nervousness wouldn't show. He got in the backseat and rode along in silence, worried about giving away his identity. He knew if the Nazi found out who he was, a Jew, he would have probably had him killed.

This was just one of the many harrowing experiences he had, but, through them all, he never gave up. The driver dropped him off in a small village near Budapest, where he set off for the city. By now it was the middle of December 1944. Everyone was living in the ghetto.

He didn't know where to find us or whom he could turn to for information, but he found his way back to the apartment building where we had lived with Grandma and Grandpa. There, he met one of our gentile former neighbors who told him of our whereabouts.

She told him that we were in the ghetto, near the entrance gate, where she had seen us. But he was unable to make contact with us until after the war.

In the meantime, he didn't want to risk being caught and deported again, so he concentrated on staying hidden. Wherever that might be at any given time, he felt better, at least to be in the same city as us. One day, he went to his manufacturing plant, now run by his partner, where they came up with an idea. The workers fabricated a metal box, like a small trunk barely big enough to fit one man, which they hoped would go unnoticed if left in the industrial area next to the plant. Now containing your father, they placed it in a vacant lot, adjacent to a cemetery. He paid one of the gravediggers to bring him food at night and, for over a month, he remained locked in that tiny box in the freezing cold, almost paralyzed. He didn't see the sky again until liberation on January 18, 1945.

As mother described my father's survival solution, it seems hard to believe that a person could survive all that time cramped up in a tiny box. How did he breathe? How did he sleep? How did he stay warm? Did he have a blanket? With all these questions running through my head, I kept thinking about my father's personality and his iron will to live. Where there's a will, there really is a way — my father was proof of that.

Mother continued:
I know he had some type of blanket, but how much good it did I don't know. He used it both as a bed and as a cover. I know the box was small, not even long enough for him to stretch out or turn on his side. I think he stood up to stretch only when the gravedigger came with the food and opened the box. As for breathing, I think they had punched some holes large enough for ventilation, but small enough to avoid suspicion.

While his survival and tenacity ware amazing, I will always wonder.

The one crucial lesson to learn from all this: despite the hatred that surrounded us, many brave and decent people tried to do the right thing. Thanks to them, our family survived that horrendous war. And, because of their bravery, more of us are alive today to tell our story.

Although your father's partner helped us survive the war years, his wife, Agnes, had a different mission. The only information that was circulated was Nazi propaganda, and many people believed that everything stated in the newspapers or on the radio was true. A few months before we were captured and taken to the ghetto, Agnes came to Grandma and Grandpa's apartment, supposedly to help. She warned me that the Nazis would soon find us and take us away for good, but that your father, who was in a labor camp, would probably return. She suggested that we give her some of your dad's clothes so he would have them when he came back.

I was outraged by her assumption, but I had enough sense to hide my anger and mistrust. Instead, I told her that I had already given everything away. What I had suspected turned out to be true. This woman was an informer who was hoping to benefit from our predicament and get some of Dad's clothes. Within hours after she left the apartment, four men appeared at the door. Two of them wore Hungarian Arrow Cross uniforms, one wore a police officer's uniform, and another was in civilian clothing. To see if I had told the woman the truth, the men searched through the house. I was very fearful, as many people had been deported or killed for lesser crimes. I had no way of knowing what else they were really looking for, and what the consequences could be. During the search, they did find a suitcase full of important personal belongings — jewelry, papers, and money, which they seized and took with them. They must have been satisfied with what they found because they left without harming us. We were relieved and safe — at least, for the time being.

However, that scary episode spawned an amazing turn of events. It turned out that the man dressed as a civilian was actually a detective, and, from the papers they took that day, he was able to track us down a few months after liberation. He claimed that he had helped us during the raid by persuading the Nazis to leave us alone after they found the suitcase and that he was coming back to us now because he needed our help. He said that his wife had left him, and that he had been dismissed as a detective. After having helped so many people, including us, he now needed our help in return. Your father didn't think twice, and gave him a job on the spot. He worked for us for almost three years, and it felt good to finally be able to help someone else.

Chapter 6

LIBERATION

The liberation of Hungary was not an overnight process. It was slow and bloody. The Nazis put up a strong resistance. The Russians had to go from building to building, street to street, and town to town. Budapest was a large city, where there were many bitter street fights. At first, I was afraid to even go out because I didn't know what I would find. It took days before many of us found the courage to venture outside of the ghetto. Still hearing sporadic gunshots, I didn't want to risk my life or yours by taking you out. And I definitely didn't want to leave you in the apartment with anyone.

"For a few days I stayed in the building, but when I stopped hearing gunshots fired and people came back to reassure me that it was safe to go out, we left. Still, we were worried. Just because an area was liberated did not mean that we could move around freely. It took some time until the whole city was secure. Luckily, the Russians moved fast and the chaos did not last long. Within *ten days, the city was freed — the Germans and Hungarian Nazis were gone. Three months later, on April 4, 1945, the whole nation was declared free from German occupation. It was a time of great joy.*

As liberation from the Germans became a reality, the old laws and restrictions were lifted, political fears diminished, and our thoughts turned to family. We wondered if our loved ones had survived, in what condition, and when they would get back. We hoped and dreamed of seeing them again.

Most of us wanted to return to where we used to live. I didn't know if Grandma's old apartment building was standing, or even if it was safe, but I took a chance. Not only did we find the building intact, but we were welcomed by Grandpa, who had arrived shortly before us. Neither of us had known about the other's whereabouts, although we had both been living in the ghetto. We had a thankful, tearful reunion. You were still very ill, once again with pneumonia, so my joy was overshadowed with worry and concern. But we managed to get medication, food, and shelter and, fortunately, over time, you got well. I was grateful and amazed that you, a one-year-old child, had been able to survive so much sickness and under such horrendous conditions.

Even though we were now free to move around, I did not leave the apartment until you felt better and I felt safe. We spent most of the time cleaning up, finding supplies, and searching for food and heating materials. We had to fix all the broken windows. It was the middle of a cold winter and time to begin preparing for the future.

We were grateful to be living without the constant fear of bombs exploding nearby or having to walk the streets wearing the yellow star of "shame." It took time to adjust to freedom, and to stop being fearful of imprisonment or death simply for being Jewish.

However, for many families, liberation was bittersweet. Everybody, Jews and Christians alike, had been separated from loved ones for years — and many were only now discovering that some of their family members did not survive. Entire families had been destroyed, along with property, homes, and spirits. It took a long time before people could begin to put their lives back together. Parts of the city and its streets were filled with debris from collapsed structures, and other buildings were either bullet-ridden or beyond repair. Some buildings were only partially ruined, but people were afraid to walk inside for fear of collapse.

As we settled in, we lived with the hope that our family members would return from the camps or wherever they were hiding. It was a time of great uncertainty, but also filled with hope. I wondered about your father, what happened to him. Had he stayed in Budapest or — where was he?

A few days later, much to our great joy, your father arrived. He had waited a few days — not wanting to take any chances — before leaving his metal box. Finally, he felt it safe enough to come look for us at Grandma's apartment. It was an amazing reunion. We could hardly believe the three of us were finally together again. But the anxious wait for my mother and two sisters and the rest of our families continued.

Now, we couldn't wait to move back into our old apartment. But there was a problem. During our absence, other people had moved in. It would be months before they left, and, before they did, they stripped the apartment to its bare walls.

When a former neighbor, who had lost her husband and whose home had been taken over by Russians, needed help, I felt compelled to offer her and her child a roof over their heads. Again, living with another family was difficult, but it was important to share, and we could not turn away someone in need. They lived with us for a few months, until the middle of July 1945, when we heard the sad news that the family who had once lived on the floor above us perished in Auschwitz. That left the place available for the woman and her child.

As life slowly returned to the city, people tried to put their lives together, but the shortages continued. Basic necessities and food were difficult to find and there were no trains, gasoline, or trucks to transport them. So, your resourceful and creative father found a horse-drawn cart and, together with his brother, traveled to the country. Whatever little money the two men had left from before the war, they used for their first trip to purchase food, which the peasants were eager to sell them. After traveling from village to village, they brought back enough to feed us, and some extra to sell as a way of making money.

While in the country, they had also investigated how to profit from their efforts, in addition to feeding our family. For one thing, they learned that the locals were making soap and that they needed lye for the process. So, on his return to Budapest, your father made a business contact from whom he was able to buy the needed chemical. The country folks were thrilled with their newfound source, and, on your father's next trip to the region, he and your uncle negotiated a great deal of food in exchange for the lye, as well as a big supply of soap.

During this time, we waited anxiously every day, hoping for Grandma and my two sisters to return. They had not been heard from since that horrible day at the soccer stadium. My father and brother were now living alone in Grandpa's apartment and, even though we had to walk for almost an hour to get there, I cooked for them every day — placing the food in the bottom of your baby carriage. During those daily walks I would cry, thinking and worrying about my mother and sisters. It was so painful to see women in their general age range, and wishing it were them. I refused to give up hope for their return.

Finally, after three interminably long months, your grandmother and two aunts appeared. By that time, most of Germany and Poland had been liberated, including the infamous concentration and labor camps. They told us of their ordeals at Ravensbruck and Bergen-Belsen concentration camps in Germany. It was truly a miracle that they had survived.

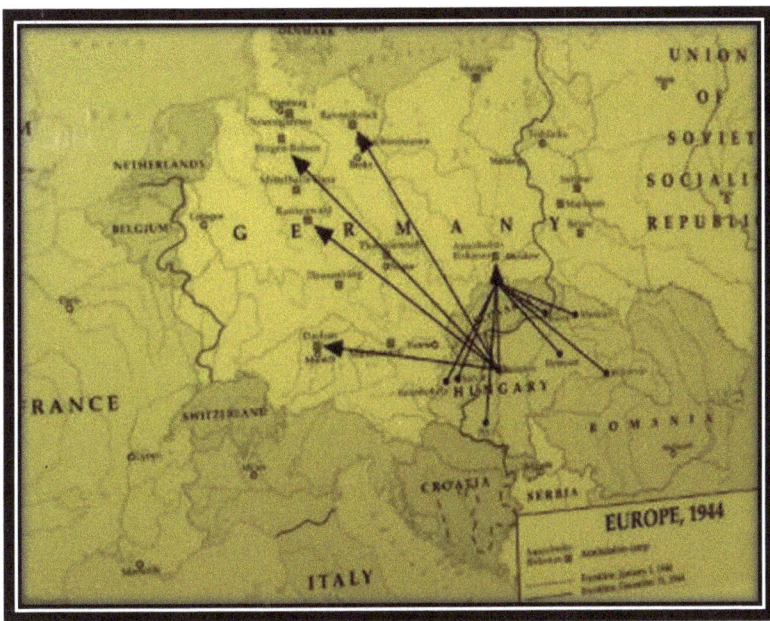

Their return journey proved a great hardship on their already weakened bodies. With trains still not operating, they had walked by day and taken refuge in bombed-out or deserted buildings at night — always cold and hungry. Many of those who had survived the camps could not endure the return trip in their weakened condition, and tragically died along the way. Hope and anticipation kept Grandma and my two sisters alive.

Reaching the outskirts of Budapest was hard enough, but with transportation not yet completely restored, they tried to run most of the way toward the apartment. When they got close, however, they began to slow down, and even stopped — consumed with fear: would they find anybody alive?

Some distance from the apartment, by some miracle, a former neighbor recognized them and gave them the good news that the rest of the immediate family was alive and anxiously awaiting their return. They burst into tears of joy and resumed their run toward the apartment. Completely exhausted, they collapsed a short distance from our building. A little later, gathering all their strength, they were at our front door. Seeing them again was such a tremendous relief; the tears of joy flowed from everyone's eyes. It took some time before the reality sank in that all of us were alive.

I was fortunate that all of my immediate family had survived. Your father was not so blessed. He had a very small family, and half of them did not return. His sister, Maritza, and her five-year-old son, Peter, were burned in the gas chambers at Auschwitz. His older brother's wife, Manci, lost the child she delivered in Auschwitz.

The story of Manci's child was a sad one. She was already pregnant when she was taken away from her hometown in July of 1944 and she delivered the baby in Auschwitz under horrific conditions. One of the inmates in her barrack was a doctor, who offered to deliver the baby under one condition: that Manci not utter a sound. Manci promised her silence even though she knew there would be no anesthetic. When the time came, she went into labor, and as promised, she muffled her cries. Following the delivery, the doctor wrapped the baby girl in paper to suffocate her, and immediately disposed of her in the trash. The child could not utter a sound, or the birth would have been discovered, and Manci, the baby, and perhaps the whole barrack would have been killed.

She never talked about this, but many years later she related the story with great difficulty, filled with emotion and sobbing. She was never able to have another child and always wondered how different her and her husband's lives would have been if their little girl had lived.

Chapter 7

AFTER THE WAR: IDYLLIC YEARS

Hungary didn't waste time developing a new era of healing wounds, finding freedom, and building a new future.

The years from late 1945 to 1949 were wonderful and promising. But even though the Nazis were gone, it was a strange and unnerving time for everybody. People tried to restart their shattered lives as the feelings of sadness and horrible memories mingled with the taste of freedom and high hopes for the future. By 1946, life was more stable, and we were anticipating a stimulating and culturally enriching life, which we hoped would provide a solid foundation for our future.

Everybody moved forward with much hope, feeling that after what we had gone through, nothing would be too difficult to handle. New businesses sprang up and thrived, and my father began to rebuild his own business. He reacquainted himself with his old contacts, while new ones sought him out to purchase his merchandise. His customer base was essential, but manufacturing and servicing were problematic due to the lack of supplies.

Mom and Dad worked together in the business; their talents complemented one another. During a medical checkup at a hospital, mother met a woman with whom she developed a close friendship. During one of their conversations, the woman revealed that her husband was the head of a company that manufactured all the chemicals Mom and Dad needed in the business. Through this woman, supplies and raw materials became more readily available.

With renewed government and non-government contacts, once again, all official buildings and public transportation vehicles were equipped with our fire extinguishers. Slowly but surely, the business once again flourished and, by 1948, my father had reestablished himself as a successful business owner.

Dad always had brilliant timing, and, knowing that times had changed, he chose to rename the business. "NOVARA" had represented the old world, and he needed a name that would represent the new. So he changed the name to "UNIVERSAL," which would represent him globally and make him well known in other parts of the world.

We lived in one of the most desirable neighborhoods in Budapest, which, to this day, remains one of the nicest — close to the beautiful Danube River. The area was filled with architecturally beautiful apartment buildings in the Classical, Baroque, Gothic, Renaissance, Art Nouveau, and Hungarian Romantic styles. Our home was on the third floor of a four-story modern building and was beautifully furnished.

My father, wearing glasses, and his brother, Pista, seated in our living room. That's me between them.

Me sitting at the piano

A Bösendorfer grand, the Rolls-Royce f pianos, stood in the hallway. I loved playing with the keys. Mommy played the piano and I often sat with her, patiently listening to the melodies.

The buildings were surrounded by large landscaped areas and parks filled with flowers and greenery — tranquil places where I spent many happy hours of fun, with Mommy pushing me on the swings or just sitting and playing in the sand. Most people lived in apartments, so going to the park was a daily ritual, which meant getting together with friends.

At that time in Europe, dinner was a light supper. The main meal was at lunchtime and usually consisted of soup, a main course like chicken paprikash, stuffed cabbage, wiener schnitzel or breaded veal cutlet, and usually ended with a yummy dessert. Another popular dish was goulash, which could be prepared in the form of a soup or a stew.

Due to the shortage of meat, many dishes called for a vegetable substitute, such as mushroom paprikash, prepared the same way, but with mushrooms replacing the chicken. Stuffed cabbage was another hearty dish because the meat was mixed with rice to make it a more complete meal. The same was true for shredded cabbage or sauerkraut, or pickled shredded cabbage. Wiener schnitzel was a staple in Hungarian cooking, fried crisp and served with parsley potatoes and a cucumber salad. This was similar to the Swedish cucumber salad, but made with onions. The salted cucumbers and onions are squeezed after a few minutes and then kept in a water/vinegar/sugar brine before serving. A sprinkling with paprika makes it a lovely presentation.

One of my favorite places was the tennis complex — a large square block of tennis courts, where I spent a lot of time with my father, who played regularly. During the winter months, courts were converted into an ice-skating rink.

I was too little to catch the balls, but I loved running around while Daddy played tennis. Still, I played with the balls and often got red clay stains all over my white clothes. In Hungary, tennis courts had red clay surfaces, not cement/concrete or grass. Mommy would get upset with me because the stains were difficult to wash out. Daddy tried to teach me tennis, but I found the racket too big and heavy. People used to say, "The racket is bigger than you are." I put off playing until I was bigger than the racket.

My parents loved to entertain and spent a lot of time with friends — sometimes they got together just to talk, other times they played cards. There was no television. Everybody wanted to share good times together, to make up for the lost years. Mommy always served beautifully and set the tables with gorgeous linens. Most of their friends did the same.

In Hungary there were no caterers; we lovingly prepared our food at home. Mommy prided herself on serving a sumptuous buffet that was delicious as well as a feast for the eyes. Since we ate our main meal at lunchtime, the evening meal was usually light — such as a selection of open-faced sandwiches. There was a huge variety made from various breads, cold cuts, and vegetables — served buffet-style. Beautiful, colorful, and tasty.

Creating a selection of open-faced sandwiches was time consuming, because these were not simple little sandwiches, but a wide range of elegant creations made by cutting a baguette on the diagonal into thin slices, then topped with flavored spreads and cold cuts. I loved to nibble as we were making them. A favorite was a popular spread called *korozott*, made with cream cheese, butter, lots of paprika, mustard, and chives, spread fairly thick and topped with slices of radish or green pepper for color. Everyone loved its slightly tart, piquant flavor. These little sandwiches were then decorated using a pastry bag and tips, filled with toppings of various colors and flavors made from sour cream or cream cheese, and colored light red from paprika or pale green from finely chopped chives. Guests often asked to be invited back. "We love everything you prepare. When can we come for supper again?"

Desserts were not only a delicious ending but also an important part of the meal. They represented our sweet life, a life of freedom. Mommy loved to bake and prepare fancy desserts, which she learned from a friend who owned a specialty bakery. Under normal circumstances, chocolate was not available, but my mother was able to purchase it through her friend.

She enjoyed baking so much that she even had our kitchen built with all the professional equipment and a special section for my size, with a marble tabletop just like hers.

I liked watching and helping with the sandwiches, but I really loved assisting with desserts. I spent many happy hours at my own kitchen space with Mommy and our cook, mixing and rolling dough. I couldn't wait for Mommy to make the delicious and beautiful marzipan fruits, which she served alone, or, sometimes, as cake decorations.

Marzipan fruits: usually a clove for the stem or green marzipan.

Of course, I always sampled everything. Many cakes started with a mixture of eggs and sugar, then beaten egg whites. Hungarian pastries were various types of sponge cake. Some yellow, others chocolate, and usually made with cocoa powder, not with chocolate. Chocolate was not readily available for baking purposes, as it was mostly in ready-made confections. I loved to lick the bowl, especially when it contained chocolate. Mommy let me do just about everything, except place the pans in the oven. The oven was part of a big gas stove, and the door was heavy. After I burned myself once, she said, "Until you grow up, I will have to do that for you."

For me, the hardest part of baking was using my small hands to fill and hold the big pastry bag. I used to squeeze too hard and, instead of going on the bread or cakes, the mixture would spill out all over the table and make a big mess. If it was chocolate, I had a chance to lick the bag, so I practiced it a lot until I learned how to use it.

My favorite cake was made with two sheets of chocolate cake and a mousse-like filling, made with chocolate folded into whipped cream. Melted chocolate was poured on top, and when the chocolate set, it was cut into squares. Yummy, yummy!

Cooking and baking were like my playtime, and I had a lot of fun. Mommy always told me, "The food has to look as beautiful as it tastes," so I learned to do it right. I cut pastries using a ruler, to make sure that every piece was exactly the same size. People would tease me, but I wanted my pastries to look exactly like the ones Mommy made.

One time when I was busy making dough, I added too much flour. With a deep breath I blew some of it away. My dark hair became white and I almost choked on the flying flour. Mommy rushed to pick me up, and tried to blow off the flour, so I wouldn't breathe in any more of it. Cleaning up was a chore, but at least I didn't get yelled at. I never blew on flour again.

Cooking and baking were not as easy as they are today. Shopping had to be done daily because there were no refrigerators, only a small icebox. The iceman came to our street daily with his cart, and filled our icebox. There were no supermarkets, so every item had to be bought in a different shop and prepared and cooked daily. There was a bakery for bread, a dairy shop for all the milk products and eggs, a greengrocer for fruits and vegetables, the butcher for meats, and a specialty shop for cold cuts and delicacies.

Although Aunt Rosa did not live in, she was with us most of the time, and was in charge of the household: shopping for food, planning our meals, and coordinating other part-time help. There were no washing machines, so everything had to be done by hand. One person came in to wash the clothes, and another to iron them. Someone else came to do the heavy work every few months, like window-washing and cleaning the rugs. Life was quite different in those days, which is why we appreciate living in these great United States today, with all the luxuries that we take for granted. What a difference — living in Europe in the forties and fifties and living in the U.S. in the twenty-first century.

Public transportation was excellent back in the mid-twentieth century, and the population was accustomed to it. Few people had cars in those days. They were considered a luxury. We were among the lucky ones. We had a beautiful touring car, similar to today's limousine. I loved it, and so did all my friends. Neither Dad nor Mom drove. We had a chauffeur, Bela, who didn't live in, but spent a lot of time with us.

Sitting on the back of the car, Mother with sunglasses standing by

I loved to cook and bake, and go to school, too, which gave me a chance to be with lots of children my age. At my nursery school, we sat at small tables and chairs, and spoke only English. We not only learned to read and write, but we were also taught manners, table etiquette, and social graces. My parents taught me to eat properly with a knife and fork, and the school made sure we did it well.

We had lots of toys to play with, and we did a lot of coloring and cutting paper dolls. When it wasn't raining, we played outside in the big playground. School was in the mornings, after which Bela and Mommy would pick me up. Some afternoons we went to the park or did errands with Mommy. But many times she stayed home to prepare food for a party that evening. Sometimes I stayed home to cook and bake with her, or else I spent the afternoons with Daddy. It was always a big decision. Should I stay home with Mommy or go with Daddy? He worked in the mornings and was usually free in the afternoons to spend time with me.

Every day Daddy would go to the famous coffee house, Savoy, where he got together with his friends. They talked a lot, smoked cigarettes or cigars, and played cards. They also drank espresso and ate cake. Daddy always ordered me my favorite hot chocolate and a piece of cake. I loved all the cakes and had a chance to eat a different one each time. I also loved sitting on

Daddy's lap, watching the grownups play. Some days one of his friends brought along his daughter. She and I would bring our dolls and we had lots of fun playing. Not too many fathers took their daughters to the Savoy coffeehouse. It was very special. All the waiters made me feel like a princess.

Daddy loved dark chocolate, and his taste for it rubbed off on me. Every day he would take me to a nearby chocolate shop for a yummy treat.

I liked to do all sorts of things, and especially loved going to the factory with Daddy, where some of the workers always had a special treat for me. My parents' business included exhibiting the full line of fire extinguishers at trade shows, and they would often take me with them. Wherever we went, people knew Daddy and respected him. I remember often asking, "How come everybody knows him?"

I loved watching Mommy dress every day in her beautiful clothes and jewelry. It was exciting when she put on her perfume and spayed a little on me. I also loved to dress up. All my clothes were made for me — not only dresses and coats, but even pajamas and hats. In those days ready-made clothes were not readily available, so most people had seamstresses and dressmakers, and had everything made to fit. I couldn't wait to go to the special children's dressmaker and be around beautiful clothes. I still remember many of my outfits, especially one of them — a matching dress, coat, and hat in navy blue wool. The coat lining and collar, the dress's bow, and the hat's pompom were all made of white, navy, and red plaid taffeta. I am wearing this outfit in my parents' favorite photograph of me.

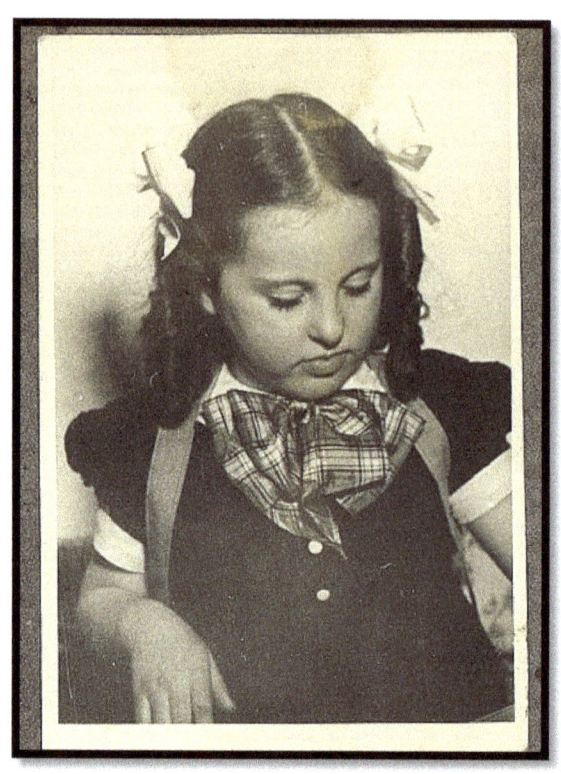

 I couldn't wait for summer and being outdoors. My parents and I spent summer every year at a favorite resort, called Csillaghegy, which translates to Star Mountain. We used to go there by car, but there was also a train ride that took about half an hour. We spent the whole summer season there with many of my parents' friends and their children.

 Csillaghegy was a special place, with three large public swimming pools — each one unique. One was a deep, Olympic-sized pool for good swimmers, another for average swimmers, and the third was a shallow pool with an artificial wave-making machine, which felt like real ocean waves, but without the salt.

 After swimming, we used to sit on the balcony eating ice cream and playing cards. I could count and read the cards, so I joined in with the older kids. We played canasta, which was a new game in Hungary at the time. We also played a lot of rummy, but canasta was more special. There was one older kid named Robert, Robi for short, who was more willing to play with me than some of the others — and he always let me win.

I spent a lot of time with my parents and other adults engaged in grown-up conversation, but, contrary to custom, they never sent me out of the room. Often, when they had political discussions, I didn't understand the issues so I asked them to explain. They gave me brief answers, which they always asked me to keep to myself; it was for our family only.

Conditions once again began to deteriorate politically, and my parents realized we needed to leave Hungary. We had to be careful about what we said and with whom we spoke. They didn't want me to know the extent of suffering that existed in the world, and the problems brewing on the political front. One of the most difficult things to explain to me was that we could not speak freely; we had to use what was commonly called "flower language" — a form of code, prearranged with relatives or contacts. For example, since our name was Fekete (which means black), whenever correspondence or conversation involved us, that word was used, but in the form of a color. Or, if a date had to be arranged, they would say that on that particular day someone was expected to give birth. Although they tried to shelter me, when they gave explanations, they were careful to tell me only what they felt was important for a child to know. They recognized the problems facing Hungary, having been through a form of it once before, and they felt the only solution for a better future was to leave at an opportune time. Unfortunately, there was no opportune time in the near future. Despite the risk, we tried to escape, but like a nightmare, we were captured and arrested on the spot.

Chapter 8

POLITICAL CHANGES

Communism affected our lives drastically, but it didn't happen overnight. I wondered how my parents were able to see the warning signs of what was to come.

At first, the changes were slow and subtle. But by 1948 the Communists had won substantial political power. While we were thankful that the Soviet Union liberated us in 1945, three years later they turned our postwar good life into one of severe, state-controlled domination. They changed laws, brought in new ones, and arrested people to silence the opposition. It began with all-day propaganda announcements on state-controlled radio stations and newspapers denouncing the capitalists' exploitation of the workers. Within weeks this gave way to the government illegally appropriating businesses, the process known as nationalization — and promising to give workers more than they had before. Of course, the promise was never kept, nor was it ever intended.

Eventually, everyone had to work for the government in one way or another, and everybody made the same amount of money. Small business owners were forced to give up their ownership and location, and were forced to become simple workers in centralized government-controlled facilities known as collectives. The managers and supervisors were government-appointed party members, mostly without much previous experience. The authorities instituted additional daily propaganda sessions in factories where they not only promoted the Communist dogma and its virtues but threatened those who opposed the process. The country's system changed from capitalism to socialism. In capitalism, businesses are privately owned, whereas under socialism the government is in control and the former owners become employees. Of course, everybody was afraid to speak out, as vocal opponents were not only arrested, but often killed. Socialism was soon followed by Communism. Those who declared themselves Communists were given power and security for the future, and promised great improvement in the quality of their lives. Party membership became extremely significant, an essential ingredient for a better life.

Because of all the atrocities the Nazis had committed against them, and with Russia liberating them from their Nazi oppressors, many Jews became loyal party members. Considered enemies of the previous regime, the Communist Party gladly accepted them. But communism was so contrary to my father's beliefs and, since he was a well-known figure, he knew he would not be accepted. Father was a businessman, in charge of his own destiny.

The Communists declared that the only people qualified for leadership were those who didn't have a "bourgeois" background. Laborers, landless peasants, and intellectuals who had been previously "exploited" by the rich were now trusted and groomed for higher positions. Former businessmen were distrusted. Power was placed in the hands of inexperienced people whose only qualification was their loyalty to the Communist Party.

Despite the Communists' promise of a classless society, a whole new class of people emerged. Interestingly, those who were appointed to high positions began imitating the behavior and lifestyles of the former upper class.

At the same time, life for the rest of us in Hungary was becoming more and more restricted and degrading. Isolated and forcibly closed off from the West, we were not allowed to read books by Western authors or listen to popular Western music, because it was considered "decadent" or "reactionary." Western movies were banned. We could not travel abroad, nor have any foreign money in our possession. Merely owning or handling foreign currency was considered a serious crime. Art that did not depict the glory of socialism was also declared decadent and unacceptable. Anything that represented Western lifestyle was forbidden. Ballroom dancing to Western melodies was stopped and, instead, people were forced to learn country music and country dancing. Now, living in freedom in the United States, it's hard to believe that political changes could alter life so drastically.

We certainly didn't have much choice but to learn to live within the limitations cruelly and forcefully imposed on us. Little by little, private enterprises ceased to exist, and opportunities dwindled for those who attempted to remain independent of the Party. I recall my in-laws complaining that on Robert's first attempt to get into dental school in 1952, he was refused because his father owned a small dental laboratory in addition to working as a dentist. Thus, he was considered an "exploiter," a person who didn't work in a collective. My father-in-law tried to retain the laboratory as long as he could, but he realized that the only way Robert would have a chance was if he closed it down and joined a collective. Reluctantly he gave it up, hoping that this would enable Robert's admission. Nothing was for sure, but after waiting several months, and losing a whole year, he was accepted into dental school.

It was amazing that my father was able to hold onto his business and renew his contacts in all the ministries. He hoped his connections would provide him protection or at least give him warning if trouble was on the horizon. These people worked in various capacities in government offices and were very loyal to Dad, but their positions were not secure. The political atmosphere was constantly changing, and we were always fearful where it would go.

We felt the pressure closing in on us. The first significant impact Communism had on our personal life was when they closed the nursery school I attended. The school's only crime was that the curriculum was taught in English, and its philosophy leaned toward Western thinking. This was unthinkable and not permissible. When the school closed, despite the risk, Mother arranged for a tutor to come to the house to continue my English lessons in secrecy. We prayed that no one would find out and report us to the authorities. I was only four years old and Mom and Dad had to explain the danger and the importance of keeping it confidential. I learned to keep secrets very early and always listened to what my parents said. It didn't always make sense to me. Still, I had no choice but to accept whatever they said.

The "single party" politics was rapidly growing, and conditions were deteriorating daily, particularly for those with a bourgeois background. We were automatically considered to be in conflict with the regime, and not to be trusted. Since my father was a manufacturer and labeled an "exploiter," we were placed in that anti-regime category, and subsequently our lives became unstable and uncertain. We never knew when and what the next restriction or decision would be, or who would be affected. The number of Dad's contacts dwindled, and those few who remained were no longer in a position to help. We soon became as vulnerable as everyone else.

Although we still lived in our beautiful home, we knew it was only a matter of time before some envious person in power might want it for himself. We kept saying, "We cannot be careful enough. We must watch every word we say — and, more important, to whom we say it." Congregating illegally, speaking to the wrong person, or saying the wrong thing was a serious crime. Receiving communications from the West, listening to Radio-Free Europe or holding foreign currency in your hand were serious offenses. People were arrested and interrogated without much real cause. We had to be particularly careful because my aunt and uncle — my mother's sister and brother — had managed to escape to Austria earlier, in June 1949, when the borders were more relaxed. They were now living free in Vienna. Having relatives in the West automatically placed suspicion upon us. We had to communicate with them through a code language, which was risky, and we feared our conversations would be intercepted. For no valid reasons, people were being arrested for their political views or for having an opinion on anything that was different from the official line.

So many people were unhappy and fearful and wanted to leave the country, but it was impossible to obtain passports legally. Just applying for one put them in jeopardy and placed them on the "undesirables" list. Those who were desperate to leave tried to do it illegally. But an elaborate spy network prevented many people from escaping, and they were arrested. Some wound up in prisons, and others were killed.

Unfortunately, my parents had been unable to join my aunt and uncle when they left for Austria because my father had to complete a major export order to Egypt. He was hoping the Middle Eastern source would prove valuable to him once he was living in the West. You can imagine the magnitude of such a transaction when you consider little Hungary exporting products to the so much bigger Egypt.

Our name and business were prominent in the community, and we had to be extremely careful and think through every detail. My creative father, as always, came up with a plan. He arranged for our help to be away from Budapest during the last few days before our planned escape. He would also send money out to Switzerland, and make final arrangements with my aunt and uncle to help us with the border crossing. They had to make contact with the person who assisted them during their escape a few months earlier.

Thinking back, it seems unreal that we even took the chance, because by then it was more dangerous, and we were risking our lives.

Unfortunately, our carefully devised plan didn't work.

Chapter 9

COMMUNISM AND BRAINWASHING

Political change is introduced slowly by the government in charge, and as days go by, the power of the new order begins to take effect. Communism is not the first step. It is generally preceded by socialism, which starts with the seizure of private property and private enterprise — a process known as "nationalization." Businesses that used to be run by professional, knowledgeable owners would now be run by government appointees, who know nothing about the businesses. This frequently ended in failure and the company's demise.

It is important to note that the slogan of Communism could be heard everywhere in Budapest. The Communists claimed that it was a one-class society where everybody was equal. However, the leaders had privileges not allowed the general population. This favoritism, in effect, made them rich and powerful while the masses had little, and remained poor. To borrow from an old saying, everybody was equal, but some were more equal than others. Legally, the leaders didn't have more than the rest of the population, but, off the record, they did. They had cars for their private use, and as much food as they wanted without having to stand in line for it. They also had telephones, which at that time was a rare commodity. Another perk was that they were also allowed to travel outside of Hungary, which no average citizen was allowed to do.

From a historical standpoint, Communism developed and changed over a long period of time, starting in the late 1800s. It began as a possible solution for the caring and providing of basic needs for the people, but, over time, it grew into a struggle for political power, resulting in the Russian Revolution of 1917. Later, following World War II, the system became all the more harsh and rigid under the influence of Josef Stalin and his enormous abuse of power. When he took control of countries like Albania, Romania, Czechoslovakia, Hungary, and Poland, he put harsh Soviet-dominated Communists in charge. With the erection of the Berlin Wall in 1961, Germany was divided into separate East and West sectors. In some places one side of the street was West and the other became East — completely cutting it off from the rest of the city. The Wall separated many families, who could not see or visit with each other until it came down in 1989, when East and West Berlin were finally reunified. This was the beginning of the collapse of Communism in Europe, at which time many countries that had been forced into joining

the Soviet Union declared their independence and became separate countries again. Russia was the biggest. I am sure you learned in geography class that the map of Europe is different today than it was before 1989. The exception to the Eastern-bloc countries was Yugoslavia, where Tito, the leader, adapted a more moderate form of communism. Today, Yugoslavia is restored to the several countries it had been prior to Communist Rule.

Several Independent countries In Eastern Europe that used to be part of the Soviet Union (in gray)

Various forms of communism still exist in several countries, but they are not united by a common border or led by a central governing body like they were in Europe. China is an interesting country. Politically, it is ruled by a Communist regime with rigid control over the people. However, financially, they have flexibility due to their massive manufacturing network and desire for success. As long as people do not discuss politics, they are allowed to prosper. North Korea is totally opposite. They are tightly controlled in every way, and the leader lives extremely well while the general population is starving.

Currently, Cuba is politically rigid but allows for a little free enterprise, in order to support the government. Many owners of large homes converted them, at first to restaurants and later rented out rooms, like a B&B. Tourism is the first free venture toward capitalism. But change would be difficult since a majority of the population is young and has never experienced freedom.

When Hitler rose to power in 1933, he saw the Soviet Union as a prime region for long-term expansion of the German "master race." In August 1939, Nazi Germany and the Soviet Union signed an economic non-aggression pact, which Hitler used as a temporary maneuver. First, he invaded Poland, and then, in June 1941, despite their agreement, he invaded the Soviet Union. The Soviet armies were overwhelmed. Cut off from supplies and reinforcements, they were forced to surrender and retreat. Hitler expected a rapid Soviet collapse, but he had not considered the strength of the country rallying to beat the enemy, and that the harsh winter conditions would create greater demand for supplies. Ironically, the Soviet army had a definite advantage in that their non-precision equipment performed better in freezing weather conditions than the German tanks and armed vehicles, which were manufactured with precision, and could not handle the harsh winter. In December 1941, the Soviet Union launched a major counterattack, driving the Germans out of Moscow.

In the summer of 1942, Germany regained the offensive and mounted a massive attack on the city of Stalingrad (now Volgograd) and the oil fields of the Caucasus. The Soviet Army not only resisted but also surprisingly defeated and cleared the Germans out of the city. This battle became the turning point in the war and signaled the beginning of the Soviets' long retreat westward across many nations, including Hungary.

In June 1941 Hungary entered World War II as a German ally, following their promise of territorial rewards and a market for Hungarian agricultural goods. But by 1942, the Hungarian government felt that the current regime had become far too subservient to Germany, and Admiral Horthy, the Regent of Hungary, appointed a new Prime Minister to extricate Hungary from its Nazi alliance. In response, Hitler invaded and occupied Hungary in March 1944, and set up a new government. Despite the German invasion, Horthy fought to retain independence, but by October 1944 his regime was overthrown, and a new oppressive government took power — however briefly. The Russian Army steadily advanced, and, as part of a January 1945 offensive, they entered and liberated Hungary.

Since one of the Nazis' aims was to create an Aryan race by eliminating Jews, for us the liberation from Nazi occupation was a godsend. What we didn't realize at the time was that the Soviets' goal was political control of Hungary and establishing a major foothold in their quest for communist domination over Central Europe.

To reach their objective, the underground Communist Party was renamed the Hungarian Workers' Party and given an important place in the new coalition government. The Soviet-controlled Communist Party then tried to overthrow the country immediately after the war ended but was unsuccessful. While the Hungarian people were unhappy with fascism, they were not convinced that communism was the solution. In 1946, only a small group supported the Communist Party, and about 17 percent of the population voted for them in that first free election. As a result, Communist supporters, along with the help of the Communists in control of the Soviet Union, began an intense campaign to win the next election.

To achieve their aim, they focused on the Communists' heroism in liberating us from the fascists and Nazis. To build a power base, they formed political alliances with trade unions, as well as the Social Democratic Party and the National Peasant Party. This strategy increased their voting power and gave them control of several key offices. One of these, the Chief Justice in the Ministry of the Interior, became a powerful tool to change laws and silence opponents. By 1947, they had legally seized control of the Hungarian government. The multiparty system was abolished and the Communist leaders began the transition from capitalism to socialism, and their actions were not merciful. They dealt with opposition by arresting undesirables on false charges, and by holding single-slate elections.

In 1948, the Communists won the election. Their methods during the election had been questionable, but people were afraid of the consequences of speaking up against them. Once the Communists gained power, a new Soviet-style constitution was ratified, and the Hungarian People's Republic was proclaimed in August 1949. By now, postwar cooperation between the Soviet Union and the West had collapsed, and Stalin's doctrines were forcefully imposed in all political, economic, and social systems. Stalin supporters became the "new elite," gaining privileges not available to the general population.

Government-controlled newspapers and radio stations became the only source of information. Radio Free Europe, Voice of America, the BBC, and all broadcasts from other countries were intentionally scrambled and jammed. The borders were now closed by creating wide minefields and barbed wire observation towers and a strong military border patrol. Entering Hungary from the West was almost impossible, and Hungarian citizens could not leave. Only official representatives of Hungary were allowed outside the country, and, to prevent defections, even they were accompanied by appointed chaperones.

Everyone was issued an identification booklet, which had to be carried at all times. Those found on the streets without their booklet were interrogated, abused, or, in some instances, sent to Russian labor camps, from which many never returned.

When the Party's secret police unleashed its full power, those who defied the regime by speaking out or organizing opposition soon regretted it. In fact, to prevent such dissension, the Party would periodically make "examples" of certain people — by having them sent to prison, or publicly executed.

Just speaking up or congregating was a crime. This is a difficult concept to accept because we live in a free country, a democracy, and we can express ourselves freely. But Hungarians under communism were controlled in every way. Travel was forbidden. Churches and synagogues were closed down, and priests and rabbis were forbidden to preach. Religious worship was banned, and people met in small groups, secretly. A beautiful old church was demolished to make room for the communist parade ground for May 1st and other communist celebrations, which were compulsory to attend. The organizers took roll call, and if you were absent you were punished in various ways at your school or workplace.

Real history is no longer being taught, so these incredible concepts may shock young readers who are generally unaware of the suffering that continued following the end of World War II.

Fear was our constant companion during all those years. An expression developed: *csengofrasz*, which translates to "fear of the doorbell," for when the doorbell rang after 10 p.m., we knew it was trouble: usually, the secret police. Even today, having lived through those days, the sound of a doorbell late at night makes my heart skip a beat.

Many people wanted to leave the country, but legal methods were no longer an option. Those who took their chances by trying to escape often met with extreme consequences. To deter escapes, the Communists not only punished those who tried to leave, but also went after their family members who remained behind. As a result, to avoid the threat of terror imposed on their loved ones, far fewer people tried to escape.

"Equality for all" became the slogan of the Communist campaign. But rather than helping people build better lives, the political leaders chose to distribute this "equality" by redistributing existing wealth and power. The Party mistrusted those with possessions, because nobody was supposed to have more than the masses, and they seized and nationalized their factories, homes, and land. This process started with big businesses, followed by the takeover of smaller ones, and finally included the seizure of most privately owned property, regardless of its value. Individuals or families were ejected from their homes, businesses, and farmlands, and most of their personal belongings were confiscated.

The rich landowners, who did not actually farm the land themselves, were called *kulaks*. Under Party order, they were forced to leave their property altogether, or to share their homes with several other displaced families. If the government allowed these *kulak* families to farm some of their own land, they demanded a level of production that was usually impossible to achieve. If the farmers could not provide the goods required, they were punished. At times, some of them had to buy produce from other farmers just to satisfy their quota. Eventually, most were forced to give up private ownership and join a government-run collective farm, where the requirements were less stringent.

The process of nationalizing businesses was a humiliating procedure for the owners. Unannounced, two or three government officials would walk into a privately owned establishment and order the owner and his family to collect their personal belongings immediately. They were forced to leave the premises without warning and instructed never to return. These officials would then seal the entrance, and the business now became the property of the government. It was a tragedy for those who had worked hard to establish and build their businesses — to have it suddenly taken away without compensation.

The nationalization of my parents' business occurred immediately after our attempted escape. All our holdings were automatically confiscated and became government property, including our car, vacation home, vineyard, and a large apartment building.

The Communist propaganda was convincing to many. Workers did not make much money, but they were tricked into thinking they were part owners of the factories in which they worked. In reality, everybody was working for the government. No one made sufficient money, except the top officials who had special privileges.

A basic salary could no longer provide a decent living. People started to look out for their own interests, and corruption soon became rampant. Aside from working their regular jobs, people established secret side businesses, which included stealing from the collectives and/or using the facilities for their own personal use. Without permission, they helped themselves to materials and equipment that was not available anywhere else.

People who did manage to make extra money had to be very careful where they kept it and, even more importantly, how they used it. According to the Party, it was inappropriate to spend too much or live too well. In fact, private citizens were not supposed to have any "extra" money — eliminating the need for banks. Only the government was allowed to use the banking system, and for import-export purposes only. If people had extra money, they knew to keep it under their mattress.

Imagine all this going on and having no access to news of the outside world! We heard either false government-contrived information, or no news at all. All three newspapers reported the same propaganda, just expressed differently. We quickly learned not to trust anything we were told. All information regarding Parliament was withheld. We could not even go near Parliament, let alone witness any official proceedings.

Whenever we went out at night, we had to remember to return home before 11 p.m., when the doors to our apartment building would be locked. We could come and go, but we were afraid to come home after hours, because the custodian would have to open the door, and he could report us to the authorities for his own gain.

My mother had a terrible scare one afternoon when she purchased some special sweets to serve to friends that evening. Chestnut puree is a real delicacy — a sweet, mousse-like favorite among Hungarians, made from cooked, peeled, and mashed chestnuts, combined with sugar, rum, and vanilla. To serve the puree, a layer of whipped cream is spread across the bottom of the dish, followed by a generous layer of the chestnut mixture pushed thru a potato ricer. The results are thin strands of chestnut--like spaghetti, which resemble Raggedy Ann's curly strands of hair. After adding the layer of chestnut, the dish is topped with mounds of whipped cream. Delicious! The shopkeeper had put it in a lovely crystal bowl, so it would be ready for serving.

Upon arriving back home, Mother found the elevator in the building had been turned off, so she started to walk up the stairs. In her great hurry, she accidentally dropped the bowl, breaking it into a million pieces. Normally this would have been only a simple aggravation, but, under those circumstances, it was a major issue. She ran up to the apartment and brought back rags to clean up the mess before anyone could find out that she had purchased such a large amount of expensive dessert. There were those who would have gladly reported the news to the authorities to win "brownie points," which the government could have used to accuse us of living luxuriously and hoarding money — a major crime, punishable by imprisonment, torture, and public show trials. Often, we could not purchase what we wanted for fear of being considered decadent. One could be severely punished for much less.

My father's entrepreneurial efforts had paid off, but we had to be careful not to show that we had more money than we were allowed. Of course, he could not work for himself anymore; he was working for the film industry, now a government-controlled propaganda machine, which he somehow managed to operate as a private enterprise.

There were government agents spying and reporting on people everywhere — hoping to benefit their own pocketbooks or save their lives. Like most everyone else, we spoke only to close and trusted family members or friends. No outsider could be trusted. The Communists made sure no one resisted their prescribed mode of life. As a result of this insular behavior, people did not know what was going on in the country. Even close relatives could not always be trusted, often creating friction within families.

Workers and children were forced to attend regular weekly or monthly propaganda seminars, in addition to the daily school programs. At these brainwashing sessions, local Party leaders reinforced the virtues of the Party and its benefits for everyone. Roll call was taken each time, and those who were not in attendance had notations made in their government files. These negative remarks were carefully kept and collected, later used against us in all phases of our lives.

The same propaganda was fed to us in theaters and movies, at schools and universities, all of which depicted some kind of heroism or successful accomplishment of the Party. We also had to participate in regular marches carrying flags and yelling slogans. Attendance was enforced at these events, such as the annual May Day celebration, and we were required to carry placards denouncing Western imperialism, especially American policies. Sometimes, the government supplied eggs and ink bottles to throw at buildings, such as the American Embassy, which represented the free, independent society. We suffered emotional trauma because we did not support the government's philosophy.

Communist indoctrination began at a very early age. Children were taught Russian ideology and new beliefs to insure the perpetuation and success of the Party. One of the youth organizations, called Pioneers, was modeled after those in Russia. Schoolchildren had to wear uniforms of a white shirt and red kerchief. Regardless of how you felt, you were expected to participate in various daily activities, including propaganda lectures. The hidden agenda in these lectures was the serious attempt to urge children like yourself to report anyone — even your own parents — if you heard them speaking against the regime.

Unfortunately, many children did report parents or other family members. They were young and did not understand the predicament their parents were in, nor the tragic consequences of their actions. These relatives were interrogated, persecuted, and sent to labor camps or even executed. Can you imagine how these children felt when they learned what they had done?

However, they became the favored property of the government, like poster children. Many were rewarded with money or educational opportunities at Russian universities, where, of course, they were totally immersed in communist philosophy. By starting the brainwashing early, the Party believed that the children would grow up to be true Communists with unquestionable loyalty.

At home we always discussed opposing viewpoints. My parents let me listen and ask questions to make me understand the political climate and our own personal circumstances. They repeatedly instructed me not to talk to anyone outside the family about how we lived, the things we did, and especially about our political views. They made sure I understood that there were people who would use this information to ensure a better life for themselves — willing to sell their souls and put their families in jeopardy. Very early on, I learned the importance of having righteous principles, keeping secrets, and knowing that it was sometimes essential to lie. My mother and father explained the difference between *lying for survival* and *lying in general*.

One of the biggest problems facing the communists was the housing shortage. Most of the leaders of the new Communist Party had to move from the country to Budapest, the capital, where housing was in short supply. To solve this problem, the government devised a method of 'displacement and appropriation.' They simply got rid of undesirable people, like former capitalists, and took possession of their apartments. First, they falsely accused them of committing crimes against the State, and then, without a hearing or investigation, they persecuted them. Some of them suddenly disappeared and were never heard from again.

While the majority of people suffered, the new leaders were getting rich and growing fond of the luxuries of their new lifestyle.

Chapter 10

ESCAPE FROM HUNGARY

By 1949 my parents had seen the handwriting on the wall. With new laws in place, the conditions were getting worse. They knew we had to leave Hungary to avoid the next persecution, and to assure they could raise me in freedom. My aunt and uncle had successfully escaped to Vienna in March of that year and kept begging us to join them.

But we were realistic and knew that leaving would be difficult, especially for a man as prominent in business as my father. We would need more than luck to pull it off. Despite the obvious risks, in July 1949, my parents finally decided on our plan to escape. We knew our lives would change drastically and that we would have to give up everything. However, we hoped the loss would be temporary, and that we could create a better life and future in a new country, where we could live in freedom.

Knowing that money would play an important role in our escape, before leaving, we secretly arranged to send money out of the country. It was illegal to do this, but we had a Swiss bank account from prior to the war, and due to my father's import/export business, we had managed to channel money through intermediaries and business connections.

This was not a simple task. The process involved a difficult and circuitous route, and was dangerous for everybody involved. But we were desperate.

We realized that we should have left earlier in 1949, and that my father's business decision to remain behind and complete the shipment to Egypt was a grave mistake. But now, without any more delays, Mom and Dad started the wheels turning, and through various means we were eventually able to make contact with my aunt and uncle in Vienna. Our every action was scrutinized, telephone conversations were monitored, and we never knew who was watching or listening nearby. We were afraid to hand over a letter to another person for fear the exchange would provoke suspicion. Since Dad conducted an export business, he was in a better position than most to make contact with anybody outside of Hungary. But it was still a risk. When we communicated it was through code. For example, if we wrote, "Please send six yellow roses to Judy on her birthday, July 20th," it meant that on July 20th Judy took six pieces of gold jewelry.

Another line of communication was conducted through those who traveled to the West, legally. Fortunately, we had connections with artists and newspaper reporters, who were the only people allowed outside of the country. The communists emphasized the importance of international competitions, and the journalists reported on the success of our sports figures. Hungarians were outstanding gymnasts, soccer players, and ice skaters. They always had to travel in groups and were never left alone without a chaperone. One of my father's closest friends, Laszlo Lukacs, was a highly regarded sports writer with free access to the West, and he acted as liaison to my aunt and uncle in Vienna.

"Next to every big gate there is always a small door" is a common expression in Hungary, which roughly refers to those who would do anything to find a solution to difficult problems. Although it was forbidden, enterprising people made a business out of helping Hungarians escape. This involved hiring a so-called "broker," usually from Budapest, who made the arrangements with a "farmer," a local man from a nearby village, to handle the Austro-Hungarian border crossing.

The "farmer" was familiar with the guards and the general layout of the land. One person was to escort us from the train station, then hand us over to another, who would take us close to the border in a horse-drawn buggy. From there, we would cross over into Austria by foot, guided by a villager.

Using a guide was vital because the Hungarian Army had placed landmines along the border to eliminate escape attempts. The landmines, together with watchtowers, patrolmen, police dogs, and barbed-wire fences, created a dangerous no-man's land. It was Winston Churchill who dubbed this forbidden zone The Iron Curtain.

Darkness and unmarked roads made any escape attempt even more dangerous. Children were often sedated, because people were sometimes caught when the border patrol responded to a child's cry. The border was not a straight line, and people often crossed over into Austria at one point only to later find themselves back on Hungarian soil and under arrest. The worst was when greedy villagers took money from people on the false promise of ushering them across the border. Instead, they led them to the guards, who, in turn, turned them over to the authorities.

It is important to explain this because many villagers did this harmful thing not because they wanted to but because they were put into uncompromising positions. The authorities may have forced them to do it.

We not only had to worry about the crossing and the handling of our departure from Budapest, but we also had to make arrangements to send our domestic staff, Bela and Aunt Rosa, to the country — so Mom and Dad could make last-minute arrangements in private.

With great trepidation, we left our home very early on the morning of December 13, 1949. At the Budapest train station father bought our tickets. I was excited and kept asking my parents where we were going, to which they replied, "We're going on vacation for a few days." There was tension in the air, I had to stay quiet.

We left Budapest and disembarked the train late at night near Sopron, a town only about half an hour from the Austro-Hungarian border. On schedule, we met our crossing guide and, after boarding his horse-drawn buggy, we headed toward the border

Before leaving that morning, we left a note instructing Bela and Aunt Rosa to look for a letter on the piano under the lace cloth. The letter explained that we had left the country, and to take whatever of our belongings they could for themselves. Fortunately, they did this early in the day, because, by evening, when we were captured, the AVH, the State Secret Police, became aware of the situation and immediately sealed off our apartment. From then on, no one but officials could enter.

Chapter 11

CAPTURE AND ABDUCTION

The train finally stopped and we got off. It was 10 o'clock at night — cold and dark. I didn't know where we were, but I noticed my parents frantically looking up and down the platform, searching for someone. Mother held my hand as we walked outside the station toward a horse-drawn open buggy with a man standing beside it. He looked at us and called out in code, "Fekete bogar," meaning "black bug" in Hungarian. That scared me. I didn't understand the symbolism; I thought the man meant a black bug was crawling on me. But Mother grabbed my hand and pulled me away. Dad nodded at the man and said, "Let's all get on the wagon, and Zsuzsika [the endearing name for me in Hungarian], you hop on the front seat next to the driver."

Mother looked worried. I didn't understand it, but I didn't say anything. I was five years old, excited to be riding in the front seat. My parents sat in the back and, without another word, we left the station. It was scary in the freezing night air, but, tired as I was, the adventure kept me awake. I was still under the impression we were going on vacation. The only noise I could hear was the clickety-clop of the horse's hooves on the dirt road.

I had never sat in a country wagon before or even been that close to a horse. I had to hold my nose because the smell was so strong. It was a bumpy ride as we trotted along in the dark and I could not see a thing. It felt like we were in the middle of nowhere. Although we had only been riding for a short time, I began getting restless.

"When are we getting there?" I asked the driver. He didn't answer. Mommy and Daddy were silent, too. I looked around in the dark, and the only things I could see were red sparks floating around. I didn't even have a chance to ask what they were before a flashlight glared in my face. We had been trotting along the bumpy road for about ten minutes when we were halted by a cigarette-smoking guard. We stopped. I was too scared to speak. Suddenly a soldier appeared at my side, the red sparks flying from his cigarette. I looked back and noticed two other men standing at the back of the wagon. They were big and burly, dressed in dark, heavy uniforms, and holding large guns. I was the first person the soldier spoke to. The other men were talking to Mom and Dad in the back of the wagon. I had no idea who they could be, or why we had stopped.

"Where are you going?" he asked me.

I began to tremble. He sounded so mean. He kept looking at me as he puffed on his cigarette.

"Get out!" one of the soldiers yelled.

We got off our wagon, and I ran to hug Mommy. She picked me up and whispered in my ear. "I'm sorry we had to lie to you. These men are border guards [whatever those were], and we are not going on a vacation. I'll tell you more about it later."

As we stood there, we heard a noise. Another wagon rolled up next to us and ordered us to get in. Mommy quickly explained that the guards were bad people who didn't like us, and that we were under arrest.

We were still in Hungary.

As we all sat in the back of the wagon, Mommy struck up a conversation with one of the soldiers guarding us. As opposed to the others, this one seemed friendly and was willing to talk to us. He was admiring Mommy's fur coat, leather handbag and gold pin, and said that if she gave him these items, he would arrange for our release and we would be free to return to Budapest that evening. After we arrived at the police station, however, another patrolman came over, and the guard stopped talking to Mommy. They couldn't make the final agreement; the deal was off.

Inside the police station we were gathered into a large room with a group of adults and children who had tried to escape the country the previous night. We all had to spend the night there, sleeping on the hay-covered floor. Mommy and Daddy la side by side, and I laid my head on Mommy's stomach. While it was freezing outside, it felt warmer inside, but only from the collective breathing. I cuddled up to Mommy; her warmth comforted me. We were surrounded by armed guards who looked at us with so much hatred that being cold was not even important.

As soon as they finished taking our names and looking at our I.D's, I saw one of the guards pick up the telephone. They did not waste any time. I asked Mommy who they were calling. She explained that the border patrol contacted the authorities in Budapest, and the officials there immediately confiscated our home and all of our belongings. All of our real estate, as well as business and personal belongings, were seized. Gaining possession of our car, a rare item in Hungary in those days, along with our business and real estate holdings, made our capture a fine treasure for the Communist Party.

Early next morning, the guards banged on the door and woke us up. They gave the grownups coffee, which looked like muddy water, and a piece of stale bread — no butter, no jam. We children each got a watery hot chocolate and were still hungry when the guards ordered us out. They led us to a waiting bus and announced that they were taking us to a larger police station in Szombathely, a two- to three-hour drive. I clutched Mommy's hand and clung on for dear life. The women and children were kept grouped together by several guards, and the men were separated from us — their hands and feet chained together. I was so frightened and confused; I had never seen handcuffs or chains before and I started to cry at the sight of my Daddy chained to the other men. I had always spent a lot of time with my dad, and wherever he and I went, he was respected and admired. And now he looked sad and ashamed. I didn't know which was worse, the sight of him shackled to the other men, or the sound of them shuffling along with the clanging metal. I was also afraid for Mommy and me. If they did that to Daddy, what would they do to us? Mommy held my hand tight and talked in a soft voice to comfort me.

The guards made us get on a local bus, where some village people were already seated. They put the male prisoners on the bus first, then mothers with children. I sat in Mommy's lap in a seat across from Daddy. I couldn't take my eyes off him, but he didn't look back at me. I kept crying, but Mommy's hugging me made me feel safe. All during the bus ride we went without food or drink. As hungry as I was, I said nothing.

We happened to sit next to a woman who kept looking at Mommy and me with great sympathy. Mommy had a unique talent for being able to read people, and she was able to connect with them, even under these conditions. She noticed this woman's sympathetic expression and asked if she would do her a favor. "Would you contact my mother-in-law in Budapest?"

Mommy explained to the woman that Grandma Riza was probably worried, waiting for our telephone call. We had agreed to call her when we arrived into Austria. The woman was willing and Mommy gave her Grandma's name, address, and telephone number. She said, "Please tell her what you saw here, and assure her I will try to contact her after we arrive at the prison."

The woman seemed to understand and promised she would do it. Mommy thanked her and prayed that she would.

We got off the bus in Szombathely. Mommy held my hand real tight. A moment later, she squeezed even tighter, and gasped.

"What is it?" I asked.

She shushed me. From the look on Mommy's face I knew something must be wrong. Mommy was shocked to see the woman she had talked to on the bus give a big hello and a warm hug to a man dressed in uniform. She thought she had made things worse by asking for help from somebody who was possibly connected to the government. Now, instead of easing Grandma's worries, she might have gotten her into trouble as well. She realized she should have known better than to trust a stranger.

After our arrival in Szombathely, the authorities held a brief hearing at the police station. The room was sterile; walls were painted an ugly yellow-beige, with a large photo of Prime Minister Rakosi and various propaganda slogans hanging on the walls.

"Viva Rakosi! Viva the Party!"

"Reach for Socialist Victory!"

There was a large filing cabinet against one wall, and a long, light-colored wooden table and chairs in front of it, on which sat several papers and a telephone. On another wall was a washbasin with a dirty towel hanging from it. The so-called judges were two Communist officials who looked at us as traitors for wanting to leave the country. While they sat at the table, we had to stand in front of them during the interrogation.

They simply asked, "Are you guilty or not?" But they didn't even listen for a response. Our answers did not matter, because everybody who was caught and brought in was found guilty and was almost certain to be sentenced to prison.

We had known several people who, not too long before our attempted escape, were also captured, but released within a short time. So we had hopes of being released relatively quickly. That didn't happen. Of the entire group, my father and mother both received the longest sentences: twelve months for him and eight months for her.

Mother's sentence was the longest among the women because she was the official owner of a large apartment building in Budapest and considered to be the "wealthy one" among them — a serious crime in the eyes of the Communist Party. In that initial phone call, they had learned all the information they needed to know about us.

When the verdict was announced, we were shocked at the length of the sentences.

All during the hearing, I stood next to Mommy, gripping her hand. I didn't understand what was going on, but it felt serious. As the sentences were handed down, the women began to cry. Male guards appeared and handled the men, and female guards approached the women, one for each person. I didn't dare talk, but I looked around quietly. The guards held something silvery and shiny in their hands. Suddenly, a female guard appeared from behind and pushed me away so she could place the handcuffs on my mommy. I was horrified and started to tremble and shout, "Mommy! Mommy!" She began to cry and I began to sob uncontrollably. The male guards started to yell, ordering the women to move to the side. In the commotion, another female guard grabbed me and yanked me away from Mommy's side. Her hands were clammy and she smelled like that horse I had sat near the day before. All I wanted to do was run away but I could not. The guard held me so tightly it hurt. Then she shoved me to the side, toward the other children. I screamed.

Before long, all the kids were howling. From all the pushing and shoving, we screamed even louder. Not only had the guards snatched us from our parents but they pushed us into another room with the door locked behind us. We became more terrified with every passing second. Why did they take me away from my Mommy and Daddy? The guards kept yelling at us to be quiet and stop crying, but we couldn't. I could only think of Mommy and

Daddy. I wanted to be with them more than anything. All I could think of was, *Will I ever see them again?*

Chapter 12

PRISON NURSERY

The guards didn't waste any time. Almost immediately, they herded us toward the prison nursery in the next building over — an orphanage. There were six of us children, and we joined twelve others who were already there — all between the ages of three and eight. We had no idea where we were or what was going on. We were scared, shaking, cold, and screaming. The other kids, who had been there for some time, kept looking at us in silence.

The image of Mommy and Daddy shackled and chained never left me. One of the guards tried to calm us by saying, "You'll see your parents soon." I didn't believe her. She was a stranger and she was the one who had taken me away from my parents.

We were freezing and hungry, and there was no one to comfort us. The male guards at the orphanage were big and tall with mean expressions. When they spoke, they sounded angry and smelled of food and cigarette smoke. The female guard who had brought me in had sweaty palms. I wanted to get away to wash my hands.

The orphanage was one big room, with bunk beds against the walls, and low, rectangular tables with chairs in the middle. This is where the eighteen of us lived; we slept, ate, played, and survived in that one room.

On the first day, a doctor examined the new kids. They claimed they needed to keep us healthy so we would not infect the other children. After many daily exams, they lined us up and stuck needles in our arms. They told us it was a vaccination to keep us healthy. But instead of staying healthy, we all got sick a few days later — each one of us with a different illness as a result of the injections. I developed chicken pox; someone else got German measles, and the others got different diseases, anywhere from mild to serious.

Every day we were taken back to the doctor's office to be reexamined. After that first visit, I grew afraid of the doctor, and became more frightened every day. The doctor was mean; he ordered us around: "Stand here, lie down, open your mouth, turn around, go back to your room!" Every morning when one of the female guards gathered us together, I would be sobbing. The more I cried, the angrier and meaner the guard became. She would grab my hand, drag me behind her, and spank me.

We were scared, lonely, and felt neglected. And we cried a lot — missing our parents terribly. When we were not being abused, we were simply bored — with little to do to pass the time except to play with a few toys and some paper and colored pencils. We cut out paper dolls, made up games, crafted airplanes, which we threw into the air, or boats, which we floated in the washbasin. There was always a female guard watching us, looking mean and angry. She never played with us. We did no schoolwork, no writing or arithmetic. Some of the older children sat by themselves, reading and writing. If I had fun at all, it didn't last long. Thoughts of my parents in chains and other sad memories always haunted me.

All day long, the smell of food cooking in the nearby kitchen filled the air. To me it smelled awful; it upset my stomach and made me miserable. No matter how hungry I was, I had trouble eating anything. Breakfast was the only tolerable meal of the day: a watery hot chocolate and bread with lard.

Lunch was almost always smelly and mushy; usually a tasteless soup with bread, or some kind of a stew with dumplings to make it thick. It always looked the same ugly brown; even the potatoes were dark and probably old. We had no green vegetables, and rarely ate meat. Once in a great while they served breaded veal, but they would always remind us that it was a "treat." It had always been my favorite food, but not there. The yellow, uncooked look of it made me nauseous. I remembered the way my mother would serve it — crisp and reddish, with white and delicious potatoes. The others were not so bothered by the food, but for me it didn't look like anything I was used to.

Because I often refused to eat, they would sometimes threaten me, saying that I would never see my parents again if I didn't eat all of my food. Scared as I was, I still had a hard time eating. I always felt I was going to throw up. The evening meal was easier. We were served bread with lard, just like at breakfast. Sometimes in the morning we would have jam, and at night they would add scallions or green peppers with it — country style.

Bathing was another miserable experience. I was accustomed to having hot and cold running water in Budapest, and bathing three or four times a week. In the orphanage we had a bath once a week, and I wished we didn't even have that. Just one tiny tub of water was drawn for all eighteen of us, with no running water. They had to bring it in, boil it on a stove, and cool it with cold water. With each child, the ring inside the tub got darker and the water became dirtier and colder. I didn't want to bathe in that ugly, smelly water, and when I climbed into the tub I had to look away and hold my nose. They had to force me to sit down and get my face wet. The soap was a pukey color; smelled like rotten eggs and made me nauseous. Whenever I could, I got to the front of the line — to get in and out of there sooner, while it was still relatively clean. I dreamed I could somehow run away.

We hardly ever went outside because it was either too cold or rainy. Locked up inside for days, we cried all the time. Sometimes they spanked us just for crying. We pleaded for our parents, but their answer was always the same:

"If you behave and do as you're told, they will come and get you soon."

Chapter 13

IMPRISONMENT

For my parents, imprisonment was a life-changing experience.

Mother's initial inquiries about the sobbing five-year-old daughter who had been snatched from her side were cruelly dismissed. "They are in good hands," the guards said, gleefully. Some even laughed.

After they had taken all the children away on that first day, they pushed the adults, over a thousand women and fifteen-hundred men, into an empty room where they kept them — miserable, angry, frustrated, scared. They stayed in that small prison facility for ten days. All day, every day, they sat and stared at the wall, sometimes yelling out uncontrollably.

Resting or sleeping was out of the question because everyone was so cramped together sitting or lying on the floor that it was difficult to breathe. Some benches were available, but the cells had no beds. When night came, they were surrounded by the guards and forced to walk to the nearby State Secret Police prison facility. This transfer took place at night, to avoid public view.

Interrogations went on all day and night. They got little food, a single cup of coffee in the morning, and another cup of coffee at night, with some bread or a watery soup. They were starving, exhausted, and terrified — and, above all, humiliated.

Inside the facility someone had written on the wall names of attorneys who might be able to help. At that time some attorneys were still allowed their private practice, but soon after, they were all forced into State employment. Since men and women were separated, Mother didn't know when she would see Dad, or even if she would ever see him again. She felt she had to contact an attorney. There was only one telephone for all the prisoners to use, and it was hours before she was able to call and hire an attorney who would now become her only connection to the outside world.

Finally, after a few days, Mom and Dad saw each other, but neither had any idea of my whereabouts. They found out about me through this attorney, since he handled several prison cases like theirs, and was familiar with what was going on. Most importantly, at my mother's instruction, he contacted Edith Helfer, our friend from Budapest, who was also familiar with the circumstances in Szombathely. This was the same woman who, a few months earlier, along with her husband, had spent some time in the same prison for the same crime but, because of less rigid laws then, was released after a brief imprisonment.

After the attorney's call, Edith needed little explanation, and immediately departed for Szombathely to visit us. The best news she brought was firsthand information about where all the children were being kept. Her son, Tommy, had also been in the same orphanage when she and her husband were arrested. To Mother, hearing this news was the greatest relief after ten long days of constant anguish and sorrow.

While in Szombathely, Edith managed to make special arrangements to take me out of the orphanage and back to Budapest. But before they would release me the guards told her that I could not leave until I fully recuperated from an illness they refused to explain. Edith had to leave and return for me several weeks later.

I'll never forget the moment I saw Edith. I burst into tears and ran to hug her. That is when I found out that she had come for me a few weeks earlier. I didn't see her the first time; we were not allowed to leave our rooms. We never saw anybody but the guards.

Once in Budapest, I stayed with Edith for a short time. The first question I asked her was about Mom and Dad, and she reassured me they were all right. I wanted love and attention so badly that I constantly sat in Edith's lap; I didn't leave her side. After a couple of days, I calmed down a bit, and slowly became my old self again. But I became so attached to Edith that it took her attention away from her own two children. She knew that Dad's brother, my Uncle Pista, and his wife, Manci, lived near Budapest, so she made arrangements for me to stay with them. I wished I could have stayed with Edith. I felt safe with her; she had "saved" me. But she told me that their home was not big enough to accommodate me. I couldn't understand it. I kept thinking that she had rescued me, and now, suddenly, she was taking me somewhere else.

While I was living with Manci and Pista, prison life took its toll on Mom and Dad. Besides the horrible conditions, it had a tremendous psychological effect on them. The future looked bleak and hopeless because they were told nothing and knew nothing — nothing, except uncertainty. A great, dark cloud hung over them, and, as we later found out, over the whole country.

Conditions on the outside were getting worse, and more people tried to escape. The prison was full, but, as they captured more people, they kept bringing them in. To control the overcrowding, the authorities decided to move about five hundred prisoners to another facility, at the extreme eastern border of Hungary, in a town called Sátoraljaújhely. Yet another adversity to face — a long, arduous train ride. Would Mom and Dad stay together or be separated? Fortunately, they stayed together, and were in the first group to be transported out.

The guards herded them into freight cars for a day-long journey through a heavy blizzard. Men and women were separated again and forbidden to talk to each other. As before, the men were shackled and chained together, and the combined noise of the chains clanking and the clacking of the train was grating and jarring. Once they got settled inside, everybody was silent; it felt eerie. Freezing, uncomfortable, and physically and mentally exhausted, they didn't know where they were going or what the future held.

When they finally arrived in this godforsaken place, they had to walk a couple of miles from the train station to the prison. Wet and freezing from the heavy snowfall and without food all day, they were near collapse. The facility was unprepared for the prisoners. It was old and dilapidated, with no heat or blankets for anyone.

The guards jammed as many people as possible into the small cells. At least the body heat helped to keep them warm. Sleeping here, too, was out of the question. Again, no beds or bunks, and new inmates arrived in the dead of night, waking the few who had fallen asleep. In time they gave them some food. Hunger made the prisoners too weak to withstand the cold. Some people had enough guts to ask the guards if they could contact their families to have them send blankets. Surprisingly, permission was granted, and, in a week or two, blankets and coats arrived like angels from heaven.

With about twenty women in a cell, there was never a moment of privacy. The guards were vigilant in watching every move, especially with the arrival of a visitor. Everyone was suspected of smuggling in items, like cigarettes. Some prisoners made playing cards out of paper, but the guards considered that a crime, and they destroyed them. They didn't allow any diversion and repeatedly reminded the people they were being punished and were supposed to suffer.

There was absolutely no contact with the outside world. The days dragged by. At times, some of the women became delirious or hysterical from staring at the walls. One day, a guard asked if anyone knew how to embroider. Mother figured she had nothing to lose, so she volunteered and was immediately put to work embroidering slogans on small Hungarian flags. They were given to certain factory workers to keep at their workstations, considered an incentive to increase productivity. Her embroidery job put Mother in a privileged position. The lights in the cells were turned off at 8 p.m., but she was allowed to use an office to continue working as long as she wanted. This was a welcome diversion, helping to pass the time more quickly.

Dad and she saw each other only once a week during religious services, which were still allowed at that time, but were soon stopped. Other than those brief periods, they could never speak to one another during their incarceration. Jewish inmates gathered on Saturday and had a visiting rabbi for a service, while the Christians had their service on Sunday. The rabbi, as well as the priest, who risked their lives by helping us, always gave a little pep talk. But they had to be careful about what they said, because everything was scrutinized. In their cautious ways, however, they were able to pass along some information from the outside. The best part of the get-togethers was the opportunity to exchange a few words with people in the other cells.

Unfortunately, these services didn't last throughout the imprisonment because the Communists were espousing atheism, and, by April 1950, they had banned all public religious practices. Without the clergy's visits, they were once again cut off from the outside world and their confinement seemed soul-destroying and interminable.

While it seemed hopeless, they petitioned to have a hearing to reduce their sentences and were stunned when it was granted. Now, they would have to travel to a town far away, in the western part of the country. While they dreaded the horrendous train ride back across Hungary, they would do anything for a chance to shorten their prison stay.

Before leaving the prison, they were handcuffed to individual guards, a female for her and a male guard for him. The long journey began in the morning and lasted all day and night, with a transfer in Budapest. When they arrived the next morning, they were immediately taken to the courtroom for the hearing. Dad's case was heard first. Instead of reducing his sentence, they raised it, without explanation, from twelve to eighteen months. The same was true for every prisoner whose case was heard that day. So Mother assumed her fate would be the same.

While waiting her turn to be heard, she noticed a sign: "A child is the greatest value! For girls to bear children is an honor, and for women it is an obligation!" She was thrilled to discover this seemingly positive piece of propaganda. Perhaps being a mother separated from her child would appeal to their sense of compassion.

At the beginning of her hearing, as she stood before those cold, heartless officials who didn't care about anything, to their surprise, she quoted the slogan, and then asked them to release her or reduce her sentence. Their reply was a flat no. But they decided to be "generous" and leave her sentence at the original eight months. This was a significant gesture of goodwill, considering that everybody else's sentence had been increased.

As soon as the court was finished with the prisoners, the guards wasted no time in taking them back to the train station for the long journey back to prison. It was the same freezing weather and uncomfortable conditions, sitting for so long handcuffed and chained to their separate guards.

When the prisoners returned, they had no other choice but to serve out their sentences. The days went by slowly and conditions somehow got even worse, but each day brought them closer to freedom. They were increasingly worn out, losing weight from near starvation. As winter turned to spring and the weather got a little milder, they were forced to give up the minor comfort of their warm coats.

In time, as the prisoners' sentences were up, they were freed, one by one. But the miserable ordeal did not end so fast. During the release process they had to endure deplorable conditions. Only the thought of being reunited with family in Budapest kept them going. Before boarding the train, Mother called Pista and Manci to tell them of her release and to ask them to bring me to Budapest and meet at Grandma and Grandpa's apartment

Mother sobbed as she got on the train and felt like a human being again. Free, at long last.

Chapter 14

REUNITED

Auntie Manci and Uncle Pista lived in a country town about three hours from Budapest. On one of our visits there, I remember going into a pretty room that was to have been the baby's room after Manci gave birth. But Manci had lost her daughter in Auschwitz, and they never changed the room. They loved the idea of having me stay with them for a while. I think I brought a bit of sunshine into their lives.

Uncle Pista owned the main hardware-sundry store in town, and they lived comfortably in a spacious apartment. I had my own room, which looked a little like my own room in Budapest. It was already furnished for a child — with a bed, a small table and chairs, and a rocking horse. There were lots of stuffed animals and colorful animal pictures on the walls. Manci cooked a lot; she wanted to make sure I was well fed and healthy for when my parents returned. I could smell her cooking all the time. While the smell was different from the orphanage, it still reminded me of it, and it didn't agree with me. I wasn't a big eater, didn't eat many things, and any food smell made me nauseous.

A month later, on March 13th, I turned six. Auntie Manci and Uncle Pista wanted to make it special for me, so they invited their friends and a few children for me to play with. The rest of the time there were few children around, only Manci's niece, who was a year younger than me. Until the end of the school year in early June, three mornings a week I went to a preschool. The rest of the time I was usually by myself — sad and lonely for Mommy and Daddy. Manci and Pista didn't know what to do with me; nothing seemed to console me. Even going to the park didn't make me happy. I would be on the swing, and suddenly I'd burst out crying. I kept asking for my Mommy and Daddy. The separation was for such a long time, and I didn't understand when Manci said, "Mommy will be back in three months." I had no concept of time. It just seemed terribly long.

They were very strict, making certain I went to bed at 7:30 every night. I had to practice my writing and arithmetic tables every day. But no matter how well I did, it was never good enough. They were never satisfied. They constantly reminded me to use good manners and proper behavior. Not having children of their own, they did everything they thought all parents should do. They even wanted to dress me like Mommy did. They had a sailor-collar dress made for me, just like the ones I used to wear, and had professional photographs taken of me that same day, which they sent to Mommy and Daddy in prison, hoping that they would receive them. Manci and Pista tried their best and meant only good for me, but I was always longing for my parents, wishing I could be with them.

Me

Manci, Pista, and me

Manci and Pista tried to console me, but adjusting to life after the orphanage was difficult. Manci knew I loved to help set the table, so she often let me do it. They used similar china and the same silverware and water glasses as my parents. It reminded me of our home. At first, I was excited to sit down at the beautifully set table in the kitchen, but after a few days I wished I didn't have to. Eating was a daily battle.

Everything was unfamiliar to me. Manci cooked special foods but I didn't like them, and couldn't eat them. I had developed a lot of dislikes at the orphanage, and they were very intolerant of my eating habits. Their home was in the country, where people ate heavier, different foods than in the city. While Mommy and Daddy used to make me taste new things, they always let me decide whether or not I wanted to eat them. Manci and Pista gave me no choice.

They ate lots of cheeses, which were unfamiliar to me. One of them was a soft cheese that Pista spread on bread or sliced apple. He loved it, and wanted me to enjoy it, but it smelled so strong, I had to hold my nose just to be near it. He couldn't understand why I didn't like it. Manci often prepared foods that made me sick to my stomach, like chicken with the skin left on. I had never eaten it like that before; it looked gross to me. I would resist and they would become angry. Lunch was the main meal of the day and also the worst. Evening meals were easier because they were lighter, and included more familiar foods, such as cold cuts, which I liked.

Each meal became a tug of war, and I always lost. They forced me to eat every morsel. The plate always had to be left clean. They often yelled at me, looking angry and mean. At almost every meal I would be slapped or end up with a spanking, either because I had not wanted the food, or because I didn't eat it all. They did not understand that I couldn't eat their way, and they considered it misbehaving. At the end of most meals, I would vomit, and then they would punish me. I was sent to my room, and often cried myself to sleep.

Many nights I would wake up screaming, "Mommy, Mommy." At first Manci would come in to comfort me and I'd go back to sleep. But these nightmares were almost every night, so after a while they ignored it. I felt sad and alone, but I couldn't complain to anyone. I had no choice but to wait for my parents to return from prison. At times I didn't believe that they would ever come.

Then came the middle of August 1950. I was told that I'd soon be seeing Mommy. I couldn't wait for that day. I had not seen my parents for eight months. It was a long time for an adult, but it was an eternity for me. On August 18th, Pista, Manci, and I took the train to Budapest to meet Mommy at my grandparents' apartment. When I rang the bell, Mommy answered the door. I burst into tears. After hugs and kisses, she and I cried and laughed at the same time. I clung to her and didn't want to leave her side for any reason. She made me hug and kiss my grandparents, which I did, quickly, but then ran back to sit in her lap. I hugged her and couldn't stop crying. All I cared about was having my mommy back. I had so many things to tell her, I didn't know where to begin. I also had a lot of questions. Where had she been? What did she do? Where was Daddy? I couldn't forget seeing him taken away in shackles. Did the handcuffs and shackles hurt him? How long did he have to have them on? I wished he could be with us. I also wanted to know what my grandparents were doing during that time. As Mommy tried to answer my questions, comfort and reassure me, I clung to her skirt; I just couldn't get enough of her.

Manci and Pista left soon after and took a train back home. I could hardly wait to tell Mommy about living with them.

When I stopped sobbing, I told her everything. I felt so relieved. I knew that all the abuse would be over. Mommy promised to cook all the things I liked. I knew that everything would be better now that we were together.

We sat and told stories for hours. She wanted to know all about the prison nursery; what we did, what we ate, and what they did to us. She also wanted to hear all the details about Edith Helfer, who brought me back to Budapest. Then I asked her about Daddy and living in prison.

Mommy was surprised and sad to hear what I had to endure while living with Manci and Pista, but she was quick to explain that they were genuinely trying to do their best, and wanted to make sure that when we were reunited I would be a healthy, well fed child. They associated thin children with the deprivation of the war years.

Those days left me with stomach issues, and to this day I have to be careful with certain foods. The other major effect on my life that started in the orphanage was the fear of going to the doctor. Since that horrible experience, the sight of a man in a white coat is enough to make me run.

It has been seventy years since that cold December day when my mother took me to have custom-fitted arch supports made. After entering the street-front store, she removed my socks and shoes so the technician could make the plaster of Paris mold of my feet. When he appeared in his white coat I jumped up, burst out crying, and ran out of the store without my shoes or coat. My mother ran after me in a panic because it was cold and she couldn't imagine why I had reacted that way. As soon as she was able to catch up with me, still sobbing, I was able to tell her that I was afraid the man in the white coat was going to do the same to me as the doctor in the orphanage. That's when Mommy became aware of my great fear. After that she tried different strategies, but none was successful. And from then on, it was always a struggle to get me to a doctor. The agony of those days still comes back to haunt me.

While Dad was still in prison, at least Mom and I were together. But we had no place to live and everything we owned had been confiscated. We had no business, no income. We had to eat, but with what? And Mom had to find a place for us to live so she could register me for school, but where? My paternal grandmother lived alone in a lovely apartment behind the beautiful State Opera House, and when Mommy asked her if we could stay with her until we found a place, to our surprise, she refused to help. She feared for her own life, and as bad off as we were, we understood. Sheltering a dissident, someone who had attempted to escape from the country, could jeopardize one's life, even if they were family. We asked many people to help, but they all refused. Desperate, we didn't know who to turn to.

Then Grandma's friend and neighbor, Nellie, offered her home, but only for a few days. We were so grateful, we assured her that we would keep very quiet and draw no attention. Once we moved in, we kept our comings and goings to a bare minimum, to avoid the attention and curiosity of other tenants. Nellie saw that we kept to our promise and was kind enough to let us stay longer. We truly appreciated her kindness and told her how much it meant to us to have people like her.

From left: Nellie, Mother in the middle and Grandma Riza and me

Respecting Nellie's wishes was extremely important but living there was difficult. All the fear and restrictions we had to comply with were destroying us from the inside. Finally, Mother contacted her former brother-in-law, an attorney, to see if there was a way to get back the money left in our bank account prior to our ill-fated escape attempt. Although there had been a substantial balance, it was confiscated. Also, before we left, we had stashed a sizable amount of money with a friend but we could not openly use it. Because we had committed a crime against the regime, all of our assets were officially frozen and the government was legally able to confiscate all of our property. Therefore, according to government records, we could not have had any money.

Mother had to find an immediate solution to our money problems and also to solve my school situation, as this was September 1950, and I was to enter first grade. Without having legal possession of the money, we were not in a position to purchase an apartment.

Our dear friend returned our money to us as promised, but in those days, solving one problem often produced another. Mother had to make the money appear legal before it could actually be spent. So, they had to devise a plan. On the advice of the attorney, she advertised in the newspaper a collection of valuables for sale. But when people called wanting to see a particular item, she told them that it was already sold. She worked feverishly to legalize the money, get us a home of our own, and then register me for school.

At the end of September 1950, Mother managed to find and purchase a small apartment, which was actually half of a large one, divided in two. This arrangement was very common in those days. Dividing and selling half of their apartments allowed people to supplement their meager state salaries, but, more importantly, it helped to relieve the housing shortage. Politically, it was also wise to support the Communist doctrine that frowned upon the bourgeois lifestyle — the success and wealth enjoyed by a single family or individual. Our apartment was not too far from the elementary school, close to where we used to live.

Because it needed a new kitchen and bathroom, the apartment took several weeks to make ready. Then, it had to be furnished. We had nothing to furnish it with, except for a few decorative items. Buying furniture was not an easy task in Communist Hungary. Most manufacturing firms were nationalized or had gone out of business. There were, however, several so-called "National Antique Shops" in Budapest, where all the property confiscated from dissidents were sold to enrich the Communist Party. As we walked into one of these shops near our home, we were shocked to find our old furniture for sale. It was painful to have had them stolen in the first place, and now more painful and humiliating to have to purchase them back from the government. And yet, we bought some of the pieces because they offered a glimmer of light from the good old days, and a sense of home for the future. Grateful as we were to have those pieces, many were now damaged, just like our lives.

After that experience we were curious about what might have happened to the rest of our belongings. Mother found out that an important man now lived in our confiscated apartment, having moved in soon after our unsuccessful escape attempt. He was the head of the AVH, the Hungarian equivalent of the Russian KGB, and would be the country's second-in-command from 1948 to the early 1980s. While prime ministers changed often during that period, this man held onto his powerful position throughout.

We moved into our new apartment in late November 1950, constantly praying for the day when Dad would return. Due to unknown circumstances, he was released earlier than the eighteen-month sentence decreed, and on December 31, 1950, he returned home.

When the doorbell rang, we ran to open the door. The minute I saw Dad I jumped into his lap. He was weak and needed to sit down, but I didn't want to let go. I held onto his hand and sat in his lap. We just sat, talked, hugged, and kissed.

Finally, after what seemed like an eternity, our little family was together again. Now that Daddy was back, we could begin to live a normal life again. For so long, we had wondered if each of us would live or die, and now, thank God, that was behind us.

Life was now our most precious possession, but, amazingly, a few items that had held great sentimental value were returned to us by our former employees, who had bravely rescued them for us. Besides a few precious items, a photograph album was returned as well, and we still consider that to be "the most valuable treasure ever found." A few of those photos are included in the book.

I missed my Daddy so much while he was away, and, after his return, I spent as much time with him as possible. We loved to go to the Budapest Puppet Theater or walk and window shop. And I always held his hand real tight. Sometimes, I was afraid to let go.

"This is the best," Daddy would say to me, and squeezed my hand even harder. "I hope you will be my little girl for a long time."

I clung onto him like I did with Mommy when she returned from prison. On our walks, we would stop to sit and rest and enjoy my favorite ice cream or hot chocolate and a piece of delicious cake. One of my favorites was kugelhof, a coffee cake baked in a pretty shape and filled with cocoa and raisins.

Other times, I would eat gooey creamy chocolate cakes topped with whipped cream. We loved walking and eating together. It felt like those fun afternoons we had spent together before all the terrible things happened. I could hardly wait for the moment when we would stop at one of the chocolate shops and he would bring me my favorite dark chocolate candy.

    I didn't want those walks to end, but a week later I had an accident on the ice at the rink near our apartment. A big man knocked me down; I broke my leg and the special walks had to end. At first it was difficult to move around with the cast on, but after a few days I got used to it. I got around by sitting and sliding on the floor. For the first few weeks, I stayed home from school. Mommy brought home my school assignments and helped me with them. I had a lot of free time, so she also taught me to knit, crochet, and embroider. After three weeks, the doctor put on a new walking cast, and I was able to hobble around. I could now go back to school but had to stay home in the afternoons. Friends would come over to play. Four weeks later the cast was removed and I did special exercises with Daddy, who was the athlete in the family. I did different activities with Mommy and Daddy, and they were all special. I wanted to be with them all the time. I prayed that we would never again be separated.

Chapter 15

LIFE AFTER PRISON

The time Mom and Dad spent in prison drastically altered our sense of security, and by then we were living in difficult political times. We had to begin all over again. Dad was determined to succeed. After all, he knew everybody in the business; surely someone would help. However, he had to adjust and conform to the rules and regulations of the new regime. By that time, private ownership was out of the question, and since the Communists were in full force, everybody worked for the government in collectives, which were businesses that had been nationalized into government-run workplaces. Ultimately, although my father was a well-known businessman and renowned in his field, he would become just another worker for the State.

Through his connections, the Ministry of Interior issued a certificate that his professional services were greatly needed, so again he established himself as an indispensable person in the fire safety industry. An important figure, he was recognized by the government and able to operate his small business within the parameters of the regime. Mother, on the other hand, worked in a collective that manufactured small leather goods.

By now it was the spring of 1951, and we were enjoying what felt like a normal life again. Of course, "normal" was not the same as before. Our lives were seriously governed and altered by the Communist philosophy. There were so many limitations and restrictions, and always the constant surveillance. At least we were together and determined to make the best of it.

But it was only a mirage; it didn't last long. Our period of relative ease spanned only five months, from January to May of 1951. I was seven years old.

Chapter 16

COMMUNIST DEPORTATION

After Dad's return, we lived a low-key lifestyle, but under great pressure from the Communist regime. No matter how carefully and quietly we lived our lives, we were watched and scrutinized at every turn. The government kept its eye on "troublemakers" like us, even sifting through the trash to see what we had bought, eaten, and discarded. This kind of information could then be used as grounds for interrogating and eventually punishing dissidents. Threats, beatings, and the disappearance of many ordinary, innocent people increased. The secret police were everywhere and the presence of the AVH and their power to terrorize was pervasive.

Living under Communist rule, no one really knew what was going on. Everyone was afraid of everyone else; no one spoke freely to anyone, especially about politics. Growing up in the United States in freedom, you would find it hard to fathom what the leaders were planning in closed-door discussions.

Fortunately, on a visit to Hungary, I was able to secure documents that described the political goings-on — a small remnant of the prime minister's dossier.

They showed highly thought-out directives, which caused us and many others months and years of suffering, simply for the crime of being former capitalists or aristocrats. One document, in particular — the correspondence between the Prime Minister and the First Secretary of the Communist Party — outlined their plans to be carried out by their most trusted deputies.

Here is the translation of one of the documents.

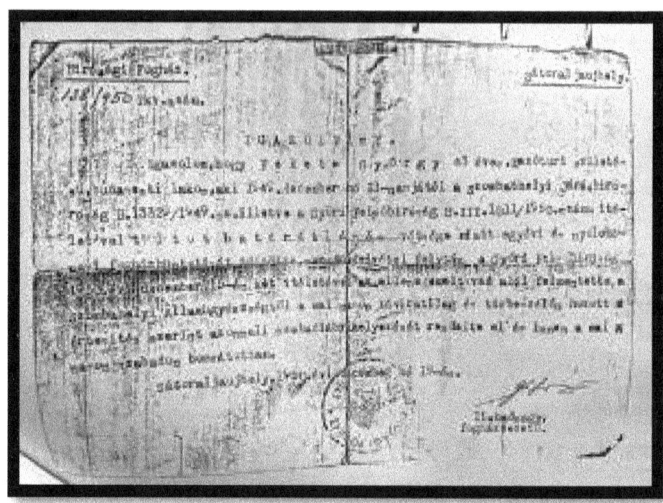

Comrade Rakosi: Highly confidential:

Attached is the committee's recommendation for the deportation process from Budapest. Regarding the displacement of undesirable people from Budapest. The transport begins at 4 a.m. and is done by truck, making two rounds of pickups. On arrival at the new location the transfer from train station to houses depends on local conditions, either by truck or horse-drawn cart.

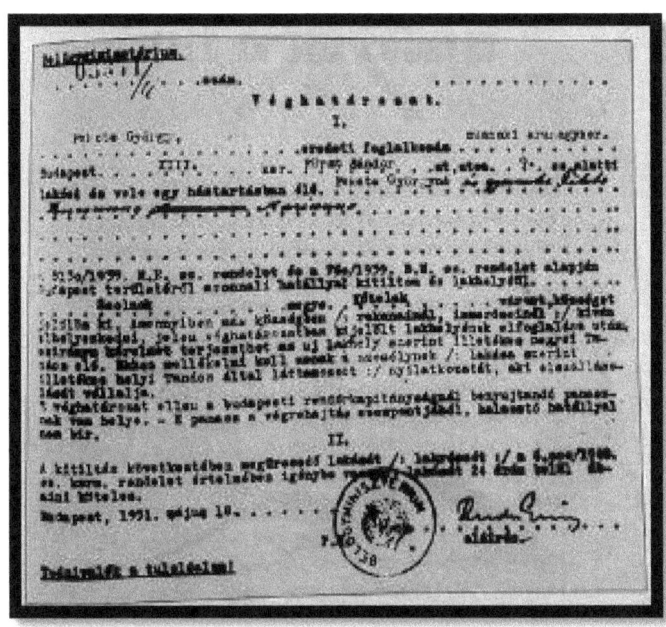

This document is the FINAL DECISION of the Ministry of Interior
It is an ORDER TO EXPEL IMMEDIATELY FROM THE TERRITORY OF BUDAPEST AND DESIGNATE another PLACE OF RESIDENCE...SZOLNOK...district...KOTELEK...town...
Complaint against this final decision can be submitted only to the Budapest Police Headquarters. In spite of any complaint, this order is final and non-postponable.
According to the...8130/1939 K.B number order and the 760/1939 number order ....
By this order of the government...your home, which is the result of this expulsion, must be transferred in writing within 24 hours.
BUDAPEST, 1951 MAY 18.................................
Stamp of the Interior Ministry...
...Signature

When the regime decided to act on the recommendations in the above documents, we were among the first forty-seven families to be rounded up and taken to a Communist internment camp. In a strange sense, it was better to have been selected on the first day because we didn't know what was going on or how bad things were going to get. Our ignorance helped us maintain hope.

We were rounded up early in the morning of May 22, 1951, and shipped to Kotelek, a tiny village of about 1,000 people. It was a three- to four-hour train ride from Budapest, then another half-hour horse-and-buggy ride on a very bumpy road. Among the other families were many aristocrats, several former high-ranking military officers and political figures from the previous regime, as well as a former prime minister. Though we were in the "best possible" company, we were the only Jewish family taken that day.

Mother had run down to the corner bakery for fresh breakfast rolls, when I heard a knock on the door. I thought it might be the custodian of the building, so I looked through the frosted glass. I was seven and alone in our apartment for a few minutes. I saw two unfamiliar men. I didn't open the door because I was instructed to never open it for strangers. The men announced that they were from the AVH, Secret Police, and they had to speak to my mother. They sounded very stern and angry. I told them that she had gone to the corner bakery and would be back very soon. I did not know what AVH meant; I just knew I was scared. I was trembling and couldn't wait for Mommy to return. They said they would slip a piece of paper under the door and go downstairs to wait for her.

When Mother returned a few minutes later, the uniformed officials greeted her with a curt command: "Gather your immediate personal belongings, leave the rest, and be ready to be picked up at 4 a.m. tomorrow." No explanation; just a note that said the rest of the information and full instructions for the deportation procedure were clearly outlined on the paper they had left under the door. When she got upstairs, I tried to tell her frantically that two men were looking for her.

She was stunned and looked tense. There had been no warning. For a minute she couldn't even think straight. We tried to understand the situation by contacting the office that had originated the orders, but no matter whom we contacted, nobody had information about what was happening. The events on the first day of the deportations came as a complete surprise to everyone — both lower level officials and, of course, the general public. None of our contacts could offer us any assistance because they were totally unaware of this new law, as were even those at the ministerial level. We were in the first group of high-profile deportees, and the process was so new that our search for answers proved fruitless.

That beautiful, bright sunny day soon turned into gloom and doom; a day filled with questions, but no answers. Realizing we could not waste any time, we began to pack, not knowing where we were being taken, for how long, or if we would ever come back. Eventually, we gathered our resources and decided to take only what we felt was most important and most precious. Imagine if you had to leave home on a few hours' notice. What would you take with you? It was difficult to think clearly, but we did our best.

We even contacted our attorney, who had become a high-ranking official in the government during the past few years, in hopes of discovering more details about the order. He didn't know anything about this ruling either, or of its consequences. However, he promised to try to find out more information and do everything in his power to help. That afternoon he stopped by the house, accompanied by another official, who told us that if we cooperated and were willing to work with him — meaning if we were willing to tell him everything we knew about everyone we knew — then this would not be a permanent sentence for us. He kept repeating that if we cooperated with them, we would be set free.

We were suspicious of his approach and did not trust his promises, so we refused his offer. "No," we said. We would take our chances. We didn't want to harm those we knew by revealing their anti-Communist sentiments or actions; but basically, we could not be certain that they would release us, even if we agreed. We figured that they would most likely have used us as propaganda tools against others to benefit their cause. The thought also occurred to us that while they might set us free one day, they might return and arrest us the following day with another false accusation.

All that day we were tense and frantic — not knowing where we were going or for how long. We also took some practical items like pots and pans and a folding bed, which turned out to be one of the best decisions we made.

Mom and Dad asked me to pack some of my belongings. As a seven-year-old, I really did not know what would be important; all I heard was, "Take very little." I packed my favorite doll and grabbed a small tablecloth that I was almost finished embroidering. I loved to draw and had many beautiful sets of colored pencils, but now I had to choose one. I picked a flat box of all the colors, which was almost new. I needed the sharpener and grabbed a bunch of paper. All the toys and games I loved, I had to leave behind. Whatever else I wanted, Mommy said was unnecessary or too big. I started to cry, but there was little they could do. They looked at each other as they tried to comfort me and said that when we got to our new place there should be a toy store where we would buy new things.

Chapter 17

LIFE IN THE COUNTRY

We didn't sleep at all that night. The sky was still dark at 4 a.m. on May 22, 1951. A truck with a very loud motor stopped outside. Few vehicles were on the streets at that hour.

A uniformed man knocked on our door. Without any formalities he simply said, "Let's go." We were ordered onto the truck with our meager belongings. The other people in the building knew something was going on but didn't dare to come out. We saw many faces watching us, hiding behind the curtains.

We were driven to a train station, where other families were gathered, waiting at the poorly lit platform. The government had worked swiftly before sunrise. After a quick head count, we were put aboard a train with hard wooden seats, ready for a three- to four-hour journey. At the next train station all of us were taken by a horse-drawn wagon to an unnamed village.

Upon our arrival, a uniformed official addressed our group of about eighty people. He explained that they would treat us well, despite our unacceptable behavior toward the Communists. We all looked at one another confused, stood perfectly still, and spoke in hushed, worried tones.

As I listened to the roll call, I heard the names of the other deportees — former royalty and important former ministers and officials. There was a prince, a princess, counts, countesses, barons, baronesses, and other honorable so-and-sos — only a few of the names sounded typically Hungarian. We were one of only three families without a title.

Hungary had once, long ago, been a kingdom. The first king was crowned in the year 1000, and the political landscape had changed many times since then, as a result of royal neighbors waging wars and conquering territories. However, despite the shifts in power, their descendants remained major landowners and retained their titles. Until the roll call, we didn't know the identities of the other people in the group. The list sounded like the Who's Who of the former Austro-Hungarian Empire. Many of the names were familiar to us from history, and here, suddenly, we were meeting their descendants. One of the women, for instance, had a brother whose face actually appeared on a Hungarian coin. Also, among the deportees was the Countess Eszterhazi, whose family history is played out in the much-loved musical, *The Sound of Music*.

Every family was assigned to a room in one of the houses in the village. The government had ordered homeowners to take in deportees. Originally, one family had occupied these two- or three-room homes, but now a different family occupied each of the rooms.

The house to which we were assigned had two rooms and an entry hall, which was typical of the village houses. Formerly owned by *kulaks*, well-to-do farm- and landowners, the houses were larger than average village houses, and were surrounded by farmland.

Prior to this we had never been to the country, except to visit summer resorts that catered to vacationers. Our situation was made all the more difficult and uncomfortable because the villagers had no knowledge of city life, and therefore did not understand why we found it so hard to adjust.

In the beginning, we were not welcome in our assigned house. The former owners resented us deportees and saw us as intruders who made their lives cramped and difficult. At first, they didn't understand that we were victims as well, and it took a while for them to realize that we had nothing to do with the government taking away their homes. As we shared our stories with them, they understood our genuine fears and terrible predicament. Slowly, their feelings toward us changed as they began to understand we were actually good people who were equally powerless — that we were all victims of the government's abuse.

Photo of the *kulak*, his wife and other kids, me at the extreme left. Water well in the background.

In addition to the emotional stress, we also suffered from physical conditions. The houses had no indoor plumbing, no running water, which we had to get from a well outside. There were no bathtubs either, so we filled a small basin with boiled water and then added cold water to cool it down. To scrub ourselves, we used a small washcloth.

We had to be careful not to get the floor wet since it was made from straw, cow dung, and water, and had a foul odor when wet. I thought a lot about the beautiful parquet floor and rugs we used to have in Budapest. We learned to wash ourselves fast and dress quickly. It was cold and we worried about getting sick.

The toilet was also outside. I was not allowed to drink anything after five o'clock in the evening. Mom and Dad didn't want me to go to the bathroom at night. But I had to plan ahead, just in case I had to go. We kept candles and matches nearby so we could find them easily in the dark, because there was no electricity, either.

Life in the country at the time was hard work and little fun. My parents and I were together in the evenings, but there was nothing to do but sit together, often in total darkness. We talked a lot, but they would try to shield me from their true feelings. Once in a while, I caught a glimpse of Mommy crying in secret, which made me break down and cry with her. I knew how hard this was on my parents and I saw them changing. They slowly began to accept this way of life. I'd hear them say that at least it was better than being confined to prison. With their loving care and constant support, I, too, learned to adjust. I had to leave my memories of Budapest behind and get used to what we had at present.

Here in the village, we were forced to do hard manual labor for our own survival and existence. We had to work the land and endure the extreme weather and cramped living conditions.

None of our previous business and social connections had been able to prevent our deportation, but at least they were able to get Mom and Dad exempted from backbreaking farm work, while all the other deportees were forced to till the land. We did only what we needed for our own needs. Mom did all the housework, cooking and baking, and Dad brought the water in from the well, which was a huge job. He had to gather containers and carry them to the well, then pull up the water and fill them and then carry the heavy pails back to the house.

Dad was mechanical, so he helped the farmer with his equipment. Maintenance was essential because new equipment and tools were not available. This helped our kulak man of the house, and, if we needed something from him, he reciprocated.

Lifestyles varied from village to village, depending on the distance from the bigger towns. The greater the distance, the more primitive the conditions. Indoor-outdoor plumbing, hard-surfaced roads, electricity, public transportation, doctors, and hospitals were not readily available, and often nonexistent. Entertainment, arts, cultural activities, and education didn't exist.

Without electricity, life was difficult enough but even candles were in short supply. During winter especially, it was dark inside even during the day and we needed candlelight just to get around. Reading or any other activity after dark was totally out of the question. To conserve on candles, we went to bed early. And, once darkness set in, there was absolutely nothing to do. Just like the farmers, we rose early each morning for a day's hard work. Our body clocks had to adjust to the local ways.

We were not locked up in prison, but the authorities kept tight control over us. Conditions were prison-like, in that we could not go anywhere without permission, except within this tiny village. Every morning and every night the police appeared at our door with large German shepherds, making sure we hadn't disappeared.

Policemen would approach the house quietly. Then, without warning, they would enter and unleash their large German shepherds. The dogs didn't actually bite us, but their growl was scary. When they found that we actually had food, they questioned us as to how we got the money to pay for it. They did not like that we had some foods that were unfamiliar to them. We learned to live with their constant humiliating gestures.

Another deportee, a former high-ranking military officer, and his family shared the house with us. He was an angry, bitter, difficult man, even in good times — but sharing the house made his behavior far more intense.

The original owners had been moved from the main house to their summer house, which contained the kitchen, and was connected to the barn about a hundred feet away. The rest of us were assigned to the main house, called the winter house, which had a furnace used for heating and baking. The kulak's son and daughter-in-law had one room; the military man, wife, son, and daughter, another; and we ended up not even with a room, but the entry hall. Thank God we had brought our folding bed with us from Budapest, because all three of us could fit on it, so at least we had something to lie on.

Living and sleeping in the entry hall had plenty of inconveniences. Whenever anyone wanted to access the wood-burning heater or oven, they had to do it from our space. Since wood was not available, we had to burn dried corn husks, which was a terribly dirty process. The dust and soot from the oven covered our room, and it was nearly impossible to breathe or keep clean. Several times a week, it was Dad's difficult task to gather the corn husks, and after the corn was harvested, leave the stalks to dry. Then he cut down and collected them, grappling with the wheelbarrow. To make matters worse, the heat generated from our space drifted into the other rooms, but we did not even have the benefit of warmth.

With no butchers or bakers in our small village, getting food was another problem. Like the other deportees, we quickly learned to farm the land so we had something to eat. We planted vegetables, raised chickens, and helped the farmers milk cows and make butter.

Learning to fend for ourselves might have been an adventure, had it been our choice, but we were resentful because it was forced upon us. And there was no end in sight. Thankfully, some local farmers taught us what to do, and before long we could handle small farming ourselves. Necessary chores took up most of the day, and, in fact, we never had enough daylight hours to accomplish all our work.

Washing was a big job because first we had to heat the water, and then scrub the clothes vigorously to make up for the shortage of soap. Without running water, rinsing was even more difficult because we had to empty the tub several times. Wringing out the heavy items and hanging everything outside to dry was sometimes worse than the washing itself. Ironing was another ordeal, because in those days everything was made of natural fibers and had to be ironed, even our cotton underwear. We had only one set of linens, so we had to work frantically to have them ready for use that same evening. The iron itself was a major effort and hard to handle; it was incredibly heavy, made of iron, and needed special coals for heating.

With all our limitations, our daily lives depended on what we could do for ourselves. When I first described it to Kyle, he was amazed. His response was, "Gosh, this sounds like Survivor, except it's your real story."

Baking was also a major job. Mom and the other woman baked for everybody in the house. In particular, we made a lot of bread which had become our food staple. Baking was done in the same stone oven that heated the rooms, and we had to put up with the dirt in our living space. The long work hours were exhausting and Mom and Dad tried to hide their emotions. Mommy and I often cried while we baked. As soon as I saw her cry, I would break down and cry with her. She always tried to comfort me and kept hoping this episode in our lives would be over soon.

Cooking was something of a juggling act. To save fuel, all three families had to cook at the same time. Wood was not available, and corn husks were in short supply. It was a small kitchen, originally intended to serve only one family. We ended up having one-dish meals, because there was not enough room for more than one pot per family. In fact, we had minimal cookware to work with. Each of the three families had only one shelf for storing pots and pans, dish towels, and other utensils. Despite all the cooking inconveniences, having a few of our own items made the kitchen the most comfortable room in the house.

Although we did not have sophisticated kitchen equipment, we managed to do a lot of preserving, which was a way of life in the country, and a necessity. Fruits and vegetables were seasonal, and by preserving them they were available throughout the year. We had to bring in a huge amount of dried corn for fuel, collect as many jars as we could, and boil water to sterilize them. We worked in shifts, and it took more than twenty-four hours to finish, since someone had to watch and stir the mixture all night long. As soon as the jam was ready, it had to be bottled. For the finishing we sprinkled a preservative on top, then covered the jars with cellophane and tied a string around the neck of the bottle. To complete the preserving process, we placed the jars in a basket covered with a blanket to keep them warm.

We cooked enough plum jam to last a year. At the end we were able to sell some of it to neighbors and barter with the villagers for some meat, which was scarce.

During the winter months, there were periods when, day after day, our main midday meal consisted of nothing else but bean soup and bread. We grew to dislike it after a while, but at least we didn't go hungry. We were so tired of eating the same things every day, there were times when we preferred not to eat.

Because we were being punished for our so-called crime, the authorities discouraged visitations from relatives, although sometimes they looked the other way. We depended a lot on the kindness of others, but at the same time, we had to be cautious with visitors. Grandpa, Mother's father, managed to come and see us every two or three months from Budapest and always brought supplies. This was not easy; trains didn't run regularly, and he had to be careful visiting us "enemies of the people." He always brought us either money or food products, with which we were able to barter for other things we needed: coffee, chocolate, some baked goods, and meat, which we couldn't get on the farm. It was wonderful to get regular soap and real toilet paper instead of the newspaper shreds we had to use. For the village people this was normal, but not for us. When winter came, Grandpa was unable to visit and we missed having the extra food.

While my parents worked and adjusted to this alien lifestyle, the three of us children attended the little local school during the school year. Hungary's educational system was centrally controlled, so to a large extent, it did not matter where in the country a child attended school. He or she received, more or less, the same education. Mom and Dad hoped that it would allow me to keep up with schoolwork.

I had always been a good student, and when we brought our test results home, I always received a better grade than the other two kids. While they didn't care, their father didn't like it. He was already rude to my family because we were Jewish, but getting better grades than his children increased his dislike of us. I would come home excited with a good grade and he would greet me with, "Here comes the ruination of my life — that stinky Jew."

I asked my parents what he meant. They just reassured me that he was angry at being forced to live in this place. The explanation helped a little, but I never got used to his torment.

At the end of the school year, the annual student achievements were announced. Having become the top student in my school, I was given the honor of carrying the school flag and leading the rest of the students in a ceremonial procession. When I saw the face of the mean man, I almost began to cry. At the end of the parade the kids went to their parents, and I ran to mine. They hugged and kissed me, and then Daddy took me aside. He lifted me into his arms and put me on his shoulders. He was so proud. He kept telling me what a good job I had done, and not to worry whenever that man said mean things to me. He reassured me that he was just jealous and a very unhappy man who hid behind his anger. Both Mommy and Daddy tried to cheer me up, telling me how proud and thrilled they were. Daddy said, "The best thing to do is just to keep up the good work."

Mommy said, "He will not change. If you can be smarter than him, and not show him how much it bothers you, he might stop saying those things."

The days were filled with feelings of despair and sadness. We had little privacy, and my parents kept trying to shield me from their feelings. They had many differences and disagreements, but deep down they were both aware that things could easily get even worse than they already were. There was always the possibility of being sent to Siberia, or to any unknown place for hard labor — or, worse yet, to prison to be tortured, and perhaps never to return alive. We lived in constant fear, never knowing how long the present torment would last, or whether something more horrible would follow. It was our strong faith and hope for a better tomorrow that kept us going. We were helpless, but not hopeless.

Uncertainty and primitive, harsh conditions shaped our lives. Being thrown together with members of former aristocratic families did make life a little more tolerable because we understood one another. They had no idea how to cook or take care of their most basic needs. And, since many of them were older, helpless, and disoriented, they had an even harder time than most. On the other hand, they were able to barter with the peasants some of the beautiful items they had brought from home. Beautiful linens, towels, jewelry, and furs were useless here, but at least some of these former aristocrats managed to sell them to the villagers in exchange for supplies, food, or money. With that, they were able to purchase goods and assistance from the villagers, who helped teach them the skills they needed to survive in a primitive environment.

Mother was one of the youngest women, and adaptable, and most importantly, knew how to cook. To make those aristocrats' lives just a little more bearable, Mother and I visited them and offered our help two or three times a week. It took many hours of our day since they were at the other end of the village, and we had to walk.

While they were not aloof and did not behave unpleasantly to us, their speech was more formal than ours. In Hungarian, as in most European languages, there is a formal and an informal manner of speech. Normally, friends and family use the informal, but the aristocracy always used the formal style, even amongst family members. To us, it felt very distant, but eventually we developed a pleasant, warm friendship with them.

Early one morning in 1951, about five months after our arrival in Kotelek, a policeman appeared at our door to inform us that we were to report at 8 a.m. the next morning to help the farmers harvest crops. Mother asked him if he knew who the Minister of the Interior was. He was surprised at her question, but when he answered yes, she pulled out our deportation orders, showing him the notation on the back, which stated that she worked "only by choice."

For me, the morning was the worst part of every day. Usually I was asleep and it was still dark when the German shepherds awakened me a little after 5:00 a.m. My parents would get out of bed immediately, but, as I peeked out from under the cover, I was greeted by the dogs' cold noses and bad breath. Their tongues literally attacked me, licking my face. I tried to get away from their slobbering by turning my face from side to side. The bad breath and dog odor were so vile I always felt sick to my stomach. The only way I could avoid their fast tongues was by getting out of bed. Even then, they didn't leave me alone. They probably sensed that I was afraid of them. It was very intimidating having them there, and I couldn't wait for them to leave. I wanted desperately to go back to sleep. The first day this happened, Daddy could see me trembling, and he realized my aversion and disgust toward the dogs. He sat me down in his lap and tried to explain that it was important not to fight them off because they might bite — especially since they were trained to attack. If I didn't fight them off, they might leave me alone. I had never had a dog of my own, so I did not know how to behave toward them. This was my first experience, and it was scary.

    The police certainly loved to torment us wherever or whenever they could. One time, Grandpa brought us some meat, which we tied into a bundle with some string and hung outside on a nail overnight. There was no refrigerator and the nights were cold. That night, when the police paid their usual visit, they let their dogs eat it. Whatever way they could torment us, they did.

    The policemen also amused themselves by playing pranks on us. One day they ordered one of the men with a beard to cut it off, and then, the very next day, they demanded he appear with his beard. Of course, it was only a prank and, when we complained, they just let it go. They knew if they carried this behavior too far, they could get into trouble with their superiors.

    After about a year of these episodes, Mother and the mean man decided to write a complaint letter. Surprisingly, about six months later, a committee from the government office came to the village, and we were summoned to appear before them. While the committee reassured us that these incidents would not be repeated, they also sternly warned us not to forget who we were. In the eyes of the law, we were "society's rejects," against the new "people's democracy," and were, therefore, considered a serious threat to the success of the regime. As such, the committee reminded us we had no rights and, to drive their point home, they issued an edict requiring both our families to relocate to a farm about ten kilometers from the village. This was our punishment for speaking up — another way of making our lives even more miserable.

Chapter 18

REMOTE FARM

On the appointed day, an official horse-drawn buggy transferred us and all of our belongings, including the chickens in a crate, to another farm that was also under government control. Similar to the way it was done in the village, the regime displaced the owners from their houses, and reassigned the deportees.

This farmhouse was bigger than the one in the village, but there were many more of us living there. The mean man's family got a larger room because there were four of them, and we three ended up with a tiny one.

While life in the previous village had been hard enough, this remote farm was worse. We felt totally cut off from the world. Of course, there were no telephones and no communication with even the villagers. Vast fields separated the farms. We could use horse-and-buggy, which was not readily available to us, or sometimes borrowed bicycles, but there were no paved roads and riding was treacherous. In fact, just getting around was difficult and visiting other deportees or keeping in touch was now out of the question. We still had to gather heating materials, fetch water from a well, and farm the land. Of course, there was still no electricity, and the outdoor toilet was even further from the house than before. To make matters worse, we now lived near a rice paddy, which was a breeding ground for filthy mosquitoes.

The aristocrats had all been raised with servants, so none of them knew how to cook. Prior to our arrival, they paid the farmer to cook for them, or they simply ate bread and other items that didn't require cooking. Now they wanted us to help. In the warmer weather we all ate cold foods so that we wouldn't have to heat the stove. Cured meats and various fresh or pickled vegetables were staples in the Hungarian diet, and special favorites in summertime.

One of the most popular types of cold food was cured bacon, which was prepared in various ways. The one I liked best was a slab of fatty bacon cooked with lots of garlic, then completely covered with paprika on the outside. It was delicious and it was red, my favorite color. Our farmer made many different types of cold cuts and sausages, and we could buy them from him. We often ate them with bread, green peppers, and radishes or scallions. There were times when we had white peppers, but not too often. It was a special treat. At night, we usually just had bread with butter or lard, which was a staple farm food. Eating lard and the fatty bacon sounds a little gross today, but during that time we were glad just to have something to eat. For beverages, my parents chose coffee, and I would drink hot chocolate.

When we arrived, we were given a piece of land, which we used over and over again. First, we had to prepare the earth, turning it, and fertilizing it, and planting the seeds. We continued to raise chickens as well as grow our own vegetables. In the village, at least we had been able to buy some items, like fruit, which we didn't grow. But that was not possible on the farm. If we didn't grow it, we didn't have it. We had to water every day and watch our vegetables grow, and we had no idea how long it might be before they were ready to harvest and eat. Like everything else in our lives, all we could do was wait patiently.

Raising chickens was quite an experience. Every morning they appeared under our window, usually while it was still dark, clucking and scratching. We would have to get up and throw them food. The ducks and geese, on the other hand, had to be fed corn by hand so they would produce more meat and a large liver. We had to brace the ducks and geese between our legs, hold their necks in one hand, and push down the corn with the other. While Mom fed the ducks and geese, Dad and I stood by, fanning away the mosquitoes and other bugs. Dad and I often compared this force-feeding method to the way Communism had been forced down our throats. We always hoped that our plight would end better than that of the ducks and geese.

It was difficult to sleep peacefully. The nights were filled with the sounds of rats and field mice on the prowl. We had to get up at some ungodly hour and light candles so we could chase them away. Our room seemed to be where the rats and mice chose to huddle in large numbers. Dad and I were the mouse catchers. Since there were no traps, we had to devise a way to get rid of them. We asked the farmers how they handled it and they suggested we place some cut-up bacon as bait, and cover it with clay flowerpots, leaving space for the rats to go under. We placed a rock to elevate one side of the pot so that when the rodents went for the bait, the pot would fall down on them. Sometimes we had to catch them by hand. For some strange reason, I was not afraid.

I'll never forget what a life we were forced to live. We prayed every day for a better tomorrow.

As we live here in the great United States, such experiences as these are difficult to imagine. Sadly, they are not imaginary; we lived every moment of them in real time. Mother and I hope that by knowing of these firsthand experiences, the younger generations will better recognize the signs if their freedom is in jeopardy, and that they will be inspired to fight for its survival.

Living on the remote farm there was no school nearby, so Mother's training as a teacher came in handy. She had finished her teachers' college education before she married, but never practiced until this time, out of necessity. Without books or materials, she created a curriculum and became the teacher for the three of us children. For the first time since we met him, the mean angry man was cooperative — grateful that his children were being schooled.

There was little else to do. With so few toys on the farm, we had to create activities. Cooking and baking were like playtime. Indeed, our new life taught all of us to be resourceful. Improvisations became the source of many new recipes, which may well be the reason I seldom follow recipes, preferring instead, to create my own versions. Despite the lack of some ingredients, we made delicious desserts that tasted as good as they looked.

I spent many happy moments in the kitchen. I loved the aroma of bread and cakes baking in the oven. I loved their yummy taste even more. Mommy taught me to make many of them. One of my favorites was a breakfast roll. We spread vanilla-flavored butter on sweet yeast dough, rolled it into a long log, cut it into slices, then baked it. During the baking process, we basted the rolls with vanilla-flavored milk, which gave them a delicious flavor and created a glaze, making them look gorgeous and shiny. I couldn't wait to eat them.

My other favorite was palacsinta, the Hungarian version of crepes. They could be filled with many different fillings, sweet or savory. Most of the time we filled them with jam or a mixture of farmer's cheese, egg, sugar, lemon rind, and raisins. Palacsinta could also be filled with a mixture of cocoa and sugar, or cinnamon and sugar. I loved every variety. And I enjoyed making them as much as eating them. They needed only a few simple ingredients, which we always had on hand.

One day I was showing one of the countesses how to make palacsinta, and everyone gathered around to watch. Mommy was very proud of me and let me do everything by myself. I was too little to reach the stove, so I stood on a chair to cook, only to slip off one day and spill hot oil all over my hand. It was extremely painful, and we had nothing to put on it to reduce the terrible burning sensation. The nearest doctor was ten kilometers away. Fortunately, the farmer offered his horse-and-buggy, and drove us to town. One of the aristocrat ladies came with us to fan my hand during the ride, to help ease the throbbing. The doctor gave us creams to reduce the pain and help with the healing. He was very kind. As a kulak's son he understood what we were going through. The pain eased by the next day, and the wound healed after a week. After that, whenever I made palacsinta, someone stood by the chair and held my legs to make sure I would not fall off. I also learned my lesson and I became more careful.

We had another incredible, memorable experience one day when Mommy was making chicken soup. She cut up the meat and vegetables and filled the pot with water. Watching the soup to make sure it would not spill all over the stove, we noticed something swimming on the top. Looking closer, we realized it was a frog. We had no idea how it had gotten in there, but since we couldn't tell if it was poisonous, we had no choice but to sacrifice the whole meal. Grabbing the pot filled with all of the wonderful, precious soup ingredients, we had to dump the whole thing out onto the ground. It was just another blow to our already degraded and humiliated condition. To this day, we are not sure whether it was an accident or if someone, like a policeman, had put the frog into the water container as a prank.

We had to think fast and make something else for dinner with the ingredients that were on hand, so we quickly prepared dough for langos, a fried bread similar to Indian flatbread. Langos was made from yeast dough, rolled out quite thin, cut into 3" x 4" square pieces, and fried, then sprinkled with salt and rubbed with fresh garlic. On the farm we learned another way to prepare it. Instead of cutting it into small pieces and frying, we kept it in one large circle like a pizza and baked it. Once it was baked, we spread lard or goose fat on top and rubbed it with garlic. Both ways it was delicious. Langos was usually served with soup during the hearty midday meal. Sometimes we even ate it in the evening with tea.

Goose fat! Lard! You may be wondering how on earth we ate that stuff. In the country seventy years ago, they ate it because it was available. And even today, villagers in many countries eat differently than their urban population. In our case, we had no choice; survival meant eating what was available.

While we had hoped that moving to the farm would provide us with a little more freedom, and that there would be fewer people around to watch us, it turned out to be as restrictive as living in the village. It was the end of 1952, and there was no sign that our circumstances would change for the better. Instead, the reality of being shipped to Russia was closer at hand.

Daddy always had hopeful words, even when Mommy was having a tough time. He kept saying, "It cannot last forever. We have to keep on going." He was always dreaming that when we returned to Budapest he would find a way for us to get out of Hungary, and live in freedom.

Our prayers were answered to some degree in March 1953, two years after our deportation. Josef Stalin died, creating enormous turmoil within the hierarchy of the Soviet Communist regime.

By September, when the political infighting in Russia had finally settled down, the repercussions of the huge political shifts began to bring instability to Hungary and all of the other Eastern European Socialist countries. One positive change included the granting of amnesty for all deportees, which was like having a huge burden lifted off our shoulders. We were finally released from house arrest and allowed to return — but not to Budapest, only to the outskirts. We were not trusted to live in the city, where we might tell people what we had experienced. Remember, information did not disseminate, and people had no clue about our experiences.

Chapter 19
RETURN FROM CAPTIVITY

Since we were not permitted to live in the city, we had to establish an official address on the outskirts. But, in reality, we lived at Grandma and Grandpa's apartment, in the heart of Budapest, in secret.

No matter the circumstances, Mom and Dad wanted me to get an education and attend school, which required a registered Budapest address. This was risky, since we had already rented an apartment, and we prayed that the conflicting information would not filter down to government headquarters. I was nine when I was accepted into fourth grade in late

September 1953, almost a month after the school year had begun. The school photo below shows the kerchief we had to wear as the symbol of "Pioneers," the youth supporters of Communism.

Class photo with our pioneer kerchiefs tied around our necks

Staying with Grandma and Grandpa was a nightmare for all of us; every moment was filled with fear and anxiety. We were still under Communist rule and every time the doorbell rang we hid, often under the bed. Even within the building, we had to be careful, because any neighbor or visitor could have been an agent, and we never knew who among them might report us to the authorities.

The most harrowing incident occurred late one night when our doorbell rang. We were gripped with fear that it was the secret police. I quickly slid under the bed, and Mom and Dad ran into the bathroom to hide. They were about to jump from the second-floor window when Grandpa yelled, "Don't worry; it's okay." He had opened the front door, and nobody was there.

Then he realized what might have caused the doorbell to ring. It was raining, and the wires had probably gotten wet. Thankfully, it was only that. It took some time to collect our thoughts and calm down, knowing what might have happened had Mom and Dad attempted to jump from an upstairs window.

I was excited to be settling into school, where I made friends with many of my classmates and received frequent invitations to birthday parties. However, I could not accept any of them. My parents did not want to take the chance of being questioned about where I lived. Since the Party encouraged children to spy on people, even on their own family members, we were afraid of drawing attention to ourselves.

Without a normal social life at school, I had to find a way to make friends with children who lived outside of my neighborhood. As a little girl I had learned to play tennis, and now it might be a way to help me find friends. We asked my friend, Andras, and his father if they could get me into their tennis club on Margaret Island, a 225-acre island in that beautiful part of the city on the Danube that separates Buda from Pest. In the nineteenth century it had been a public park. but until 1900 the only access was by boat. Now, in the twentieth century, the construction of the Margaret Bridge had made it far more accessible and, owing to its therapeutic springs, the island became a major recreational area and health resort. The tennis club was mainly used by military officers and high-ranking officials of the Communist Party, most of whom came in uniform. Andras explained that only a small number of members were civilians, and they were accepted only because they were outstanding players. At twelve years old, Andras was one of the club's leading players, and he was being groomed to represent Hungary at international tennis competitions. He and his family were neither Communists nor part of the military, but he had earned special privileges because of his talent.

Andras and his family helped me become a member, and I began playing tennis at the club every day after school. It was so exciting to meet other children my age and not have to worry about discussing our residences. We all lived in different parts of the city and no one asked where anyone lived. I loved being with them. Daddy helped me to get to the club every day after finishing his workday early. He took the first bus to the club with me, then we walked to the next bus stop, where he put me on the Number 26 bus to Margaret Island. There, he would wave goodbye and say, "Be careful, and call when you get there."

I was ten years old and felt very grown up and proud that my parents trusted me to go at least a portion of the distance by myself. I was also very careful and, immediately after arriving at the club, I would call home, as promised, and let them know I was okay. Then, I would spend the afternoon practicing and doing my homework. Before leaving there, I would call Daddy to meet me at the same bus stop. He was always there on time. From there, we went home together.

All international competitions, including the Davis Cup, were played at this club. I was one of the young players appointed to be ball boys or girls during major competitions. This gave me a chance to mingle with foreigners, although they were few and far between. I also used it as an opportunity to practice my English, seizing every chance to communicate with the players directly. I continued to develop my tennis skills and began to compete. Between practicing and homework, every moment of my life was filled with activities to get ahead.

I was very good at mathematics and decided to tutor other children. Since no one had money, I didn't get paid, but people found ways to show their appreciation. Some paid me with delicious cakes, others with various goodies. One of my favorites was called kugelhoff, which was a delicious coffee cake filled with chocolate or cocoa and baked in a beautiful special shaped pan, similar to a bundt pan. Mother wasn't able to do much baking at the time, so this means of payment felt very special to me.

I was a good student in most subjects, but despite my love of music, I had no talent for singing, which often reflected on my report card with a less than perfect score. Grades ranged from one to five, with five being the best. I got fives in all my classes, except for music, where I got a four. I asked my music teacher what it would take to get a top grade. She said that it might help if I made a school presentation on the life of a composer. So, I went to work on it immediately. I knew that there would be a festival that year commemorating the life and works of Béla Bartók, the famous Hungarian composer. I did a presentation on his life and accomplishments, which was a huge success, and from that day on, I never had to worry about my music grade. I had the same music teacher the following year when I did a similar presentation. To ensure my good grade, I always offered to help her with just about anything.

While I was a much happier person than before, life in general was difficult and insecure. Our living conditions were risky and unstable. The regime did not tolerate people like us and called us "parasites." According to them, business owners exploited their employees, which caused them to be labeled. All adults had to work and children had to be sent to childcare centers, where the brainwashing began. Mother joined with Dad, through his previous connections, to work for the two film companies. They kept a low profile, both at home and at work.

From 1953 to 1956 we lived a restricted life, but at long last, if we wanted to, we were able to participate in the many cultural activities available in Budapest. Since we had lived in hiding before, we had to be careful not to stay out past 11:00 p.m. so that the building custodian who lived on the premises would not see us coming in. Also, we did not accept invitations to anyone's home. Since we could never invite anybody to our home, we felt that if we could not return the favor, it was better not to get involved.

Due to mismanagement and abuse of the system, the economy was deteriorating and manufacturing decreased. Even basic necessities were in short supply. We had to stand in line for just about everything, even basic food items, like eggs or bread. While we couldn't buy much of anything, at least we knew they were available most of the time.

There was practically no exporting to the West, so hard currency was not available for importing goods. First-quality manufactured goods were sent to Russia, while rejects or lower-grade products stayed in Hungary. Worse yet, inferior Russian-made products were sent to Hungary in lieu of hard currency payment — and only those were available. The Russians used Hungary for their economic advantage, while we lived day to day, discontented, under the weight of constant restraint.

Stalin's death three years earlier had resulted in many changes, but the political climate shifted more rapidly between March and September 1956, during the uprisings in the other Eastern Bloc countries. There was increasing talk of freedom, and a burning desire for change filled the air. Laws and rules were relaxed

General unrest grew, and a sense that change was imminent began to fill the air. As the government eased enforcement of their rules, people regained some contact with the intellectual community in the West, and Radio Free Europe was once again accessible. Accurate news began pouring in, raising even more discontent — as well as a fervor for rebellion.

Budapest had always been a cultural center, with numerous theaters and concert halls, two opera houses, the Academy of Music, and an outdoor amphitheater on Margaret Island. However, under Communist rule, artistic ventures had served as a forum for promoting Socialism and propaganda. In 1956, for the first time in many years, freedom of expression within the arts came back to life, offering people the strength to fight for a better future. Entertainment was back in the hands of the artists, which spawned a creative boom, as well as a sense of optimism.

In September 1956, a general amnesty was announced, which finally gave freedom to all former deportees, allowing us to legally return to Budapest. We quickly found a room to rent in one of the apartments in the same building as Grandma and Grandpa. Living openly in Budapest was a glorious feeling and offered us a glimmer of hope for a free and better life in the future. Although our living accommodations were meager, at least we did not have to live in hiding and constant fear. For the first time in many years we felt we were finally free.

Now, we were hoping to find an opportunity when we might be able to leave and join my aunt and uncle in Australia.

Chapter 20

REVOLUTION

Within a short time after Stalin's death in 1953, revolts had broken out in Czechoslovakia, later in Berlin, and then spread throughout East Germany. But, after only days of bitter street fighting, Russian tanks quickly and severely crushed the opposition forces.

Prompted by these events, a group of Hungarian University students organized a large meeting to be held on October 23, 1956, in front of the statue of General Bem, a leader in the fight for freedom one hundred years earlier. The students marched defiantly from the statue to a nearby building, which housed the two government-controlled radio stations. Their plan was to force their way in and broadcast their demands for reform and for the return of Premier Imre Nagy, who, due to his liberal policies, had been forced to resign from the Communist Party several years earlier.

The radio station building was protected by many Secret Police guards. When the students attempted to enter, the police tried to disperse the crowd with tear gas, beatings, and numerous arrests. When the crowd resisted, the police opened fire and killed several people, further angering and inciting the crowd. With this, the Hungarian revolution began. That night they tried to tear down a statue of Stalin, but his statue, like his beliefs, was too firmly fixed on its foundation. Returning later with more powerful tools, they leveled Stalin to the ground.

The "Bloody Revolution," as it came to be known, began as peaceful demonstrations, but quickly turned into violent riots and street battles. News of the killings spread with lightning speed to other parts of the city and the country, as workers and freedom fighters began to take over factories, weapons depots, and Soviet tanks. A new multiparty government was formed almost overnight and hopes for true political change came alive.

Imre Nagy, considered a national hero, was soon reappointed as Prime Minister. He
promised free elections as well as full Soviet withdrawal from Hungary. Newly formed "workers councils" issued an ultimatum that strikes would continue until all Russian troops left the country, and on October 30th, the remaining Red Army tanks pulled out. The people had finally won.

At 5:45 p.m. on October 23, 1956, Mom and I left the dressmaker's shop, walked outside, and found ourselves in the midst of a huge commotion. Loud, cheering crowds had gathered on the streets, and trucks were filled with excited, screaming young people waving flags and yelling: "Freedom! Down with Stalinism and Communism!" We had no idea what was going on, so we raced toward home in dread fear. The sight of trucks filled with people yelling their slogans made it all the more frightening, especially because it was dark. It reminded us of the truck that had taken us away in those pre-dawn hours in 1951. We held onto each other and tried to push through the crowds to get away from the main road and get home as quickly as possible. When we arrived, we found that Dad had also just arrived, and he was talking about what he had seen and heard. At first, we thought they were only rumors, but we soon learned that the revolution had indeed begun. I had often heard my parents reminisce about the good life we once had. They were hoping that this was the realization of their dream of a new beginning — life beyond Communism.

As the Revolutionaries gained control, many of the dreaded AVH officers were rounded up and killed. Many political prisoners were freed. For the first time in about eight years we were able to listen to the BBC and other

Western broadcasts. As soon as the country had open communication with the West, Hungary requested assistance. Radio Free Europe and the Voice of America announced that help was on the way, and encouraged Hungarians to keep fighting, which would result in the Soviet troops pulling back. In spite of repeated statements promising assistance, the West never came. The United Nations was tied up with negotiations in the aftermath of the Suez Canal crisis.

During this period, the borders were open, and many people chose not to wait for assistance from the West. About 200,000 people left Hungary of their own accord. They did not trust the shaky political conditions, not knowing when or if the promised help would arrive, and they did not want to take any chances by waiting too long.

My grandparents, who had their passports to legally immigrate to Australia, where my aunt and uncle acted as their sponsors, were permitted to leave only because the party no longer considered them contributing members of society. Their departure would relieve the country of the burden of paying their pensions. However, Grandpa had a health issue that had to be cleared up before entering Australia. We made every effort to speed up their departure, but it still took time. For those two crucial months, until they left, we could not think of ourselves.

The revolution moved us forward politically, but our period of hope was short-lived. On Sunday November 4, 1956, at 4:00 p.m., the Russian tanks returned with a vengeance. Soviet troops suppressed the revolt, Hungary's valiant fight was overpowered, and the thousands of people involved in the struggle for freedom suffered greatly. Many Hungarians died, many others were jailed, and many more were caught and taken to the Soviet Union, where they were placed in hard labor or internment camps.

Realizing that conditions were likely to get worse, an avalanche of Hungarians headed for the Austrian border. According to reports, by noon,

5,000 had crossed over safely. Although, unfortunately, we were not among them, we made preliminary steps, hoping conditions would still allow us to cross over to Austria, as soon as Grandma and Grandpa left the country.

But the Russians increased security along the borders, and by the middle of December such an escape became nearly impossible.

Living conditions became worse than ever. The streets were filled with tanks and Russian foot soldiers. We were afraid to go out. People were stopped, arrested, and taken away. Now, again, no one was allowed to leave the country. Passports were no longer issued. The laws were tightened, scrutiny increased, and life in Hungary became even more frightening.

With the situation worsening, as soon as Grandma and Grandpa left in December, we would focus our attention on our future freedom.

Chapter 21

ATTEMPTED ESCAPES

On December 10th, 1956, the day after my grandparents finally left Budapest, my parents decided it was time for us to escape. It was far from an easy decision, as we had paid dearly for our first attempt in 1949. But since the patrols and personnel at the border had not yet been fully organized, we felt there was still the possibility of escaping. Some enterprising country folk near border towns had developed a moneymaking opportunity to escort people across the border to Austria. Dad made arrangements through a contact and, without any delay, on December 13, 1956, we fled Budapest by train, and headed for the border.

Despite our high hopes, once again, our escape attempt failed. Near the border, we were met at the train station by our prearranged border-crossing peasant with his horse-drawn wagon, similar to the one that transported us in 1949. Once we had paid him the agreed amount, we began our journey toward the border, just as we did back then. However, after only a short ride Hungarian border patrol guards stopped us, arrested us, and took us to jail. Remembering our previous attempt, we wondered what would happen to us this time. Fortunately, the new regime's procedures were not yet fully in place, and they were not prepared to enforce sentences. Released a few days later, we returned to Budapest. Instead of causing us to lie low, however, this experience made us even bolder, and on January 4, 1957 we made yet another daring attempt to escape Hungary. We were betting on the border still being in a chaotic state and that this time we would succeed. But this time, our dreams were shattered even more quickly than before. They arrested us at the train station before we even left Budapest — and, again, they took us to prison. Luckily, they kept us for only a few days as there were so many people attempting to escape that the prisons were filled to capacity.

By now our hopes to escape were fading, and we did not want to press our luck. We decided that we should obtain passports and leave through legal channels. While officially passports were not obtainable, perhaps, through bribery, they might be. This time we sought out a foolproof plan. To make it all happen, though, we had to find money and a connection. The money issue was solved when Dad found a way to release some of our funds from Switzerland. In about ten days, as if by magic, the money arrived, and we felt more confident about our plan.

Mother was always a resourceful person, and this time was no exception. She requested a telegram from her sister in Australia that Grandpa was dying, and that unless we could get our passports immediately, we would not see him alive. Having come to the passport office with this telegram in hand, she used her intuition to find someone who looked like he or she might be sympathetic to a dying old man.

Looking around the crowd, she noticed a man in the distance sitting behind a desk. They made eye contact, and she walked in his direction. When she got close enough, she noticed his uniform was that of a high-ranking officer — which she saw as a blessing. She explained our situation and showed him the telegram from her sister. He listened attentively and told her that if everything she said was true, he would see to it that we got our passports as soon as possible. He promised to search for our file, which we had submitted earlier, and then notify us when he found it. Mom did not want to take a chance, so she told him that she would go home immediately and bring back duplicates of all the documents. She was ecstatic that she had had the foresight to make copies of them — just in case.

While all this seemed promising, we were still afraid that it could be a trap; it was common practice for officials to make promises and even accept bribes, and then report the incident to the authorities. And it was impossible to predict exactly what people would do; there was always a thin line between a genuine desire to help and underlying motives.

When Mother returned with the documents, it was the end of the day, and the official had already left his office. However, since his secretary was leaving now, she decided to follow her. That led Mother into a nearby hotel's pastry shop, where she noticed the secretary greeted the manager warmly. By coincidence, Mother happened to know the manager well, and, after waiting for the secretary to leave, she asked the manager if she would be willing to act as a liaison between the secretary and her, and find out the status of our passports. This way, we could have advance knowledge, and leave the country without delay. The manager said she would be glad to help — that is, for a fee. Mother asked how much, but before the manager had a chance to answer, Mother offered her 10,000 forints, which was about an average year's salary. The manager jumped at the generous offer, and they struck a deal. Her instant response led Mother to believe that the manager's close relationship with the secretary had probably helped others before her. Just like the border crossing created a business opportunity for the peasants, people in the city used their personal connections to supplement their meager incomes. She assured Mother that she would do her best to put our case in the hands of the secretary, for personal, fast attention. She added that according to her previous experience, we should receive our passports within a short period of time, but that, together with our documents, we had to submit a written declaration that we would leave everything we owned to the government.

It seemed money could talk. We could hardly believe how fast it spoke. Our passports were issued within two weeks. But then, we had another hurdle to overcome. The passports were just a half of the emigration process. We also needed exit permits. Those were not issued until the National Bank verified that all of our possessions had been recorded and paid for. For example, valuables like a gold watch had to be paid for by a certain amount of silver. Similarly, if there was a silver item, it had to be paid for by gold.

Official requirements were generally not clear; there was an awful lot of red tape. Hungarians made it difficult and uncomfortable for anyone to leave the country. The next few days we worked furiously to prepare and complete every step prior to our departure.

My parents asked me to select what I wanted to take with me. I chose all the clothes and some art supplies and needlework materials, so I would have something to work on during the trip. In my carry-on, I also took one of my most treasured silver pieces: a miniature tea set — a replica of the large one we used to have in our home.

We sorted all our belongings and, knowing we were going to start a whole new life, we selected only the most meaningful items. At the top of our list were photographs, a few basic personal belongings, and my father's stamp collection. We packed everything that didn't require special handling, so we would be ready at very short notice. Other than clothing, everything required a government release and payment. These formalities took a lot of time and patience, which we did not have. To avoid some of the valuations, we tried to declare precious jewelry as semi-precious. The stones in one diamond ring were even passed off as glass. The stamp collection required a special permit, which took a whole day for the bank to issue.

Once everything was evaluated and declared, the payment transactions took place in the offices of the National Bank of Hungary, prior to issuance of the exit permits. They would not allow us to leave unless it was done according to the strictly enforced rules. We paid all the money they demanded and exchanged all the silver and gold as they requested. The stamp collection was placed in a large envelope, on the face of which was written, "TO BE OPENED ONLY AFTER CROSSING THE BORDER." We wondered why this item was treated differently than the rest, but when we asked, they simply said, "This is how it is done." We had no choice but to accept their meaningless explanation and hope for the best. We had planned to sell the stamps in Vienna, so that we could have some money on which to live.

The bakery manager held up her end of the bargain, and on Saturday, March 16, 1957, we received advance notice that the exit permits would be issued very soon. We finished packing and scheduled the final customs appointment for luggage examination for the day prior to the train's scheduled departure. Thankfully, our luggage was approved, and we immediately shipped our belongings ahead of us to Austria.

Under normal circumstances we would never have done this, but, knowing that the Arlberg-Orient Express, which traveled between Budapest and Vienna, did not run every day, we decided to take this major risk, knowing that our exit permits could have been revoked at any time. At this point, all we cared about was being ready to leave. We also knew that circumstances could change without notice. When we thought back on it, we realized it was incredible that we were able to ship everything before we even had our papers.

When our exit permits arrived two days later, on Monday, we were prepared and able to leave immediately. The next day, Tuesday, March 19, 1957, we left on the Arlberg-Orient Express to Vienna. A glorious day in our lives and the first day on our journey to freedom!

Chapter 22

LEAVING HUNGARY

At long last, we were leaving Hungary. We were excited, fearful, and yet full of hope. The train station was practically empty, and dimly lit. The few people on the platform were all workers bundled up in warm clothes doing their jobs. We carried our personal luggage and walked until we found our passenger car. Mom and Dad were each carrying two bags. When we finally found the car, we boarded and found our reserved seats. There were few people on the train, aside from us. Since the Communist government forbade citizens of Hungary to travel outside of the country, we were the only people who boarded the train in Budapest. It was eerie. The other passengers, already on the train, were foreigners, traveling through. The train ran from Istanbul to Paris. We were scared and didn't dare speak to anyone — nor did we move or even look around. The whistle blew at 11:00 p.m., and the train began to move. Slowly increasing speed, it chugged along, leaving the dimly lit railway station behind.

Having gone through so much before this, we could hardly believe that we were finally leaving Hungary. Despite the fact that we were sitting on a foreign train, we were still in Communist Hungary. I saw the worry and uncertainty in my parents' eyes and sensed the tension. All of our failed attempts at escape had started on trains. We held our breath as the train picked up speed and powered on in the darkness.

No one spoke; the silence was deafening. The border checkpoint was ahead of us.

At thirteen years of age I had experienced so much that by now I was well aware of the potential danger. As long as we were on Hungarian soil, anything could happen. They could revoke our exit papers at the last minute or send us back to prison. My imagination ran wild and I'm sure similar thoughts were on my parents' mind. We knew that at the security checkpoint in Hegyeshalom, the last stop in Hungary, we would have to get off the train with all of our belongings for a final search by Hungarian officials before crossing into Austria. I didn't say anything to my parents; I didn't want them to know how scared I was.

There was little to do, and I wasn't in the mood to do anything. I didn't even bother opening my bag. Just sitting and not speaking during the three-hour train ride to the border made the trip seem even longer. It gave me plenty of time to worry. I stared out the icy window, though there was nothing to see in the darkness. I saw Mom nervously trying to relax, keeping her hands clasped tightly together. Dad, on the other hand, fell asleep immediately. The pressure of the past few days had finally taken its toll, and now there was nothing left for him to do but rest.

I was far from sleepy. My thoughts began to race as I sat quietly, hoping that all would go smoothly. As the train clattered along the tracks, I thought about what lay ahead at the end of the journey. Since we were forbidden to travel or even read about living in another country, I couldn't imagine what our new life would be like. We would need to adapt to an entirely different culture with a new language and customs. It would be a whole new way of life.

The train pulled into Hegyeshalom border checkpoint. We were ordered to get off the train and carry our bags with us to the border patrol offices. A few foreigners with only briefcases went through the formalities quickly. We were the only passengers going through the lengthy procedure. I didn't say a word, but I was worried about getting off and leaving our train. Would they let us re-board? What if the train left without us? I worried that the border patrol would take too long checking us out — perhaps intentionally. The wait was agonizing. We were afraid to speak unless they asked us a question. We didn't know what to expect. They could pick on anything they didn't like, according to their individual attitude. Then, without warning, one of the border guards called Dad and took him away, and a female guard took Mom and me into a cubicle. My heart leaped in my chest. We remained frozen and silent throughout a thorough body check, and then realized they only wanted to make certain that we were not smuggling anything out. The guards said nothing. Our fear turned to terror in the silence. But then moments later, we found we had passed that part of the exam.

I stood still, shaking, while they examined my parents' bags. They had to verify that everything we were taking with us appeared on the official list. All the bags had to be checked; the seals broken, and the contents examined.

After Mom and Dad were passed, it was my turn to be searched. As I emptied my bag, out came the pencil box, along with my papers and embroidery. Then, with a loud bang, a paper bag fell out containing my adored silver tea set — undeclared. Mom turned white as a ghost, and her hands began shaking. Dad stood stiffly next to her — both of them, speechless. The officer asked, "What's this?"

Looking at my mother, I sensed we were in trouble, but, for a second, I didn't know what to say. Finally, I answered. "It's mine. It's part of my dollhouse, which I had to leave in Budapest. I wanted to keep this one item; it was my favorite piece." That was not exactly true. The tea set was always in my parents' breakfront in the living room. I must have figured it would sound believable enough to the guard.

Mom managed to regain her composure, and with Dad's arm firmly around her waist, she said, "She packed her own bag. We didn't know she had brought that along." The guard said nothing as Mom continued to make her case. "She's just a child, carrying her own little treasure."

And with that, the guard let us go.

Whew! With bags in hand, we walked back to the train as fast as we could. My legs were still shaking, but I would not slow down. We boarded the train in a hurry and kept our mouths shut as we sat down — tense and holding our breath until the engine started. Even as the train began to move, I sat there without uttering a sound. I didn't know how to apologize for my stupidity. Our whole future had teetered on the outcome of my moment of foolishness. When the train finally crossed onto Austrian soil, I burst out saying how sorry I was. And, when we saw the first Austrian sign, I broke down, sobbing. Mom and Dad hugged and kissed and comforted me as I sat between them. Then we held hands and thanked God for saving us one more time. Dad kept saying, "This is time for celebration, not for crying. It's the moment we've been waiting for, for almost eight years."

As the train sped toward Vienna, Mom said, "This is truly a memorable day!"

Dad nodded, and finished the sentence, "Today is March 19, 1957, and we have just finally left Hungary. A great day, but remember how special a day this is: it's also the thirteenth anniversary of the Nazi invasion."

We looked at each other and knew that we would never return.

Chapter 23

VIENNA

We had breathed a huge sigh of relief after crossing into Austria. In another hour, we would arrive in Vienna. In the meantime, I found the train ride exciting and exhilarating. All our anxieties were behind us, and we were filled with hope and dreams of a better future. At first, even the uncertainty of a new life in a very distant land could not dampen our spirits. However, after a while, reality set in, and we began to worry. In 1948 and 1949, we had sent out the equivalent of millions of dollars for safe keeping. But these many years later, how much of those millions would be left? We would have to wait until we got to Australia to get our answer.

As we approached Vienna, the sun came up and the bright light made us forget our dark days in Hungary. At about 6:00 a.m., when we arrived at Wien Hauptbahnhof, the Vienna railroad stations, a pleasant surprise greeted us. A representative of the HIAS, the Hebrew Immigrant Aid Society, was there at the station to offer us immediate assistance. We were reminded of the humanitarian acts we had witnessed during the war, and here we were, once again, grateful recipients.

The HIAS representative escorted us to their offices, where he found us hotel accommodations and gave us some money for our daily needs. This touched us deeply, and Mother and Father immediately decided that the minute we were in a position to do so, we would donate money to this organization. We hoped that our future contribution would help to make other immigrants' lives a little easier, just as the generous donations of strangers had eased our load.

We checked into the hotel, which was simple — no frills. But to us, it felt like paradise. We expected to be in Vienna for about two weeks, so we unpacked what we thought would be necessary. And we all took showers, one by one. That was a real turning point in our lives. We were cleansed of the old and the bad, and now the new and the good was ahead of us. With that feeling of euphoria, we started to walk down the stairs. We hurried to get out onto the street and feel the joy of our freedom.

Our first evening in Vienna was such an amazing experience. For the first time in many years we saw brightly lit streets; even the traffic lights seemed to shine brighter. Store windows were beautifully decorated and filled with attractive merchandise, which was not available in Hungary. Every window was packed with colorful, unique products. And everything seemed to sparkle. We couldn't get enough. Clothing stores were bursting with fabulous new clothes, and, although we didn't have any money to buy, we enjoyed the sights all the same. People crammed the coffee houses and sat at sidewalk cafés sipping hot coffee and tasting delicious, decadent pastries. We walked the streets till we dropped.

Newsstands were filled with so many Western magazines, we could hardly believe our eyes; so few were available in Hungary. I couldn't wait to look through them. I loved clothes! I loved color! And I loved to draw!

Everything was different. Everything reflected a sense of freedom. People were dressed in such a variety of bright colors — not the gray, bleak tones common in Communist-ruled Hungary. Color, color, everywhere! And another huge difference: no one stood in line for food — and there was plenty of it. At first, we just admired the huge displays of magnificent fruits. Then, we bought some. We could not get enough bananas and oranges, both of which were new tastes to us. We ate as if eating were going out of style until we realized that from this point on, these rare and succulent fruits would be available whenever we wanted them. Our hearts were as full as our stomachs.

This was our introduction to the lifestyle of the West. It was our first taste of our new future. It felt good, knowing that people saw us as tourists, rather than criminals.

We viewed Vienna with anticipation, excitement, and a bit of anxiety. To pay for our expenses, we had planned to sell Dad's stamp collection as soon as we arrived. However, when we opened the envelope, to our great disappointment and anger, there were no stamps inside — only shredded newspaper. This was why the Hungarian officials had written, "OPEN ONLY

AFTER CROSSING THE BORDER" on the sealed envelope that originally contained the valuable stamps. Our main source of income was gone. The Hungarian government took full advantage of anyone leaving the country. I don't know why we were even surprised. With little money on hand, we now began to wonder how much of it we would find once we arrived in Australia. Would the HIAS pay for our passage, or would we need to have my aunt send that amount to reimburse them?

Much to our surprise, it turned out that the HIAS in Vienna had contacted my aunt and uncle in Australia immediately after our arrival. They had made all the travel arrangements but requested payment to cover everything. We also needed enough money for the rest of our stay in Vienna and train tickets to Trieste, Italy, to catch the boat to Australia. With no money from the stamp collection, we had to further deplete our already shrinking account.

While we were realistic with our money situation, we didn't know when and if we would ever get back to Europe, so we made the most of every moment. Cautiously, we spent little, but enjoyed it a lot.

We enjoyed Vienna, but Trieste — a lovely, busy Italian port — offered a more dramatic change from life in Hungary. Austrians tend to be more reserved, serious people, and their lifestyle and foods were similar to Hungarians. The Italians, by contrast, were friendly and jovial people who sang in the streets and always appeared to be carefree.

The food in Italy was very different. In the mornings the wonderful aroma of baked goods permeated the air, the scent quite different from any we had experienced before. There were so many breads new to us, and we could hardly wait to gobble up every one of them. Each one was better than the last, and a feast for the eye and the palate. Breads and baked goods in Hungary were delicious also, but other than the large variety of pastries, the selection was limited. During our stay in Trieste, Dad was thrilled to run to the nearest bakery every morning. He didn't speak Italian, but by using his hands and feet and putting an "o" at the end of the words, he made himself understood. He fitted in very well. Like the Italians, Dad had always been the singing optimist.

At first, I wasn't a very adventurous eater. But since the baked goods were so delicious, we were eager to sample their most famous Italian food: pasta. Pasta was not completely foreign to us, but the way it was served was new. We had eaten a lot of it in Hungary, because meat was not always available, and pasta was often prepared as a main course. However, Hungarians serve it more on the sweet side, while Italians serve it as a first course with various savory toppings. My parents urged me to try many varieties, and I loved most of them.

In Hungary, we were familiar with only one shape — the flat noodle, like fettuccine — but we soon learned that Italians enjoyed many other shapes and sizes. In fact, during our stay in Italy, we felt we had received an education in pasta preparation and the appropriate toppings for each shape and size. Every day and in various places, pasta seemed to be served differently. According to those who tried to explain it to us, the thickness of the sauce determined the best pasta to use, because each sauce would adhere best to specific shapes. Italian cooks were creative in their toppings, and even when they were simple, they were delicious. We had a wonderful time sampling all of these new discoveries. We wished we could learn more and understand better how to make some of the sauces or the delicious sweets. We were surprised that every meal began with a plate of pasta, followed by a meat course. We often wondered how, after a big bowl of pasta, people could enjoy a second course. Life seemed wonderful, and we felt like children let loose in a candy store. Everything was new, satisfying, and fulfilling and most importantly, we felt a calm that we had not experienced for many, many years.

We would have liked to be able to communicate with the people, but none of us spoke Italian. After a few days, I picked up a few basic words that helped. I learned "please," "thank you," "hello," "goodbye," and the numbers, which together with my hands helped to make simple conversation. Hearing me talk, my parents often used a phrase to express their pleasure: "You cannot be sold in Italy anymore."

Chapter 24

LEAVING FOR AUSTRALIA

Following our arrival in Trieste, the HIAS representative in charge of our group advised us that, due to immigration issues, other people were being given priority to leave before us. We resigned ourselves to waiting for the next ship, feeling as though we had taken two steps forward, and one step back.

After spending two weeks in Vienna and a couple of days in Trieste, we took a train to Genoa, where HIAS put us up in a hotel for the next month. It was the second week of April 1957, and the weather was good for walking. We did as much sightseeing as possible. I managed to pick up a little more Italian, which helped us get around more easily. To pass the time, we often played cards.

By the end of April, a little sooner than expected, we boarded our ship, the Oceania. The majority of the 500 passengers were either tourists traveling for pleasure or immigrants freely departing from Western European countries. We were part of a smaller group of immigrants, refugees, who had no experience in international travel, especially for such an extended journey. Thirty-nine of us were Hungarians.

At that time, people in Europe traveled mainly by train since distances between countries were generally not great. This ship voyage would be long, but we were so thankful to finally be on our way.

Our crossing would take about four weeks — and we would sail through the Suez Canal. Aside from our concerns and uncertainties, we were excited to be experiencing a part of history. At the same time, we were worried about being aboard the first ship to cross the Canal following the 1956 Israel-Arab War.

All of the Hungarian passengers were assigned to large dormitories: the men in one, women in another. This made us feel uncomfortable since we learned that the other passengers, the non-refugees, had their own cabins. The ship's office's explanation was that this was a more expensive ship than the one on which we were originally booked, and that the amount paid only covered this ship's dormitory accommodations. Since we did not have money for an upgrade, we were stuck. Another blow, certainly, but a small price to pay for our new freedom.

We had many pleasant experiences during the thirty days aboard ship, but the voyage also demonstrated that being Jewish made us targets in many parts of the world. Mom had told me horror stories about the war, bigotry, and the hardships we survived as Jews during the Nazi era. And now I was seeing similar things for myself.

As we were passing through the Canal, which was not yet totally cleared of the mines and wreckage from the recent war, we had an incident that brought back sad, even frightening, memories of experiences we endured over the previous ten years. Headed for the port of Aden in Yemen, our ship hit something and could not proceed. Communist oppression and lack of transparency flooded our minds, and we worried about what might be behind this latest barrier to our freedom. Not one member of the crew provided us with an explanation of what had happened. By the evening, after many long hours of uncertainty, we were able to move on.

We were greatly relieved and glad to be heading to Aden, only to learn firsthand that the Yemenites considered Jews to be their enemy, regardless of individual circumstances.

The officers aboard ship knew from the papers we had filled out that we were Jewish and specifically instructed us to keep a low profile, warning us to remain onboard while we were in port. They could not be responsible for our safety in a foreign land. We had thought that once we left Communism behind, we would not feel the threat of racial or religious persecution. But we were wrong. We had no choice but to stay onboard and miss our opportunity to visit the town of Aden, which sounded like a fascinating place with a very different culture from our own.

As we sailed the Indian Ocean, we had another unpleasant encounter — a typhoon only ten knots away from us. Typhoons are the equivalent of hurricanes: they are called typhoons in the Indian Ocean and hurricanes in the Atlantic. The force and effect of the winds were creating waves so high, they crisscrossed the ship from side to side. Most of the passengers became very seasick. The crew set up ropes throughout the ship, connecting doors and hallways, for everybody to hang onto, to keep from falling. The ship not only rode up and down on the waves, but it pitched from side to side. Never in my life could I have imagined that feeling of helplessness — of being somewhere out in the middle of a vast ocean, tossed about so wildly. My parents and I stayed together in the lounge, watching the angry ocean play out its fury. The experience was so new it felt both frightening and exciting. Fortunately, we didn't realize the seriousness of the conditions.

The dining room was shut down and passengers were served simple meals in the lounge, although the majority of people were too sick to eat. We were among the lucky ones who were unaffected. Mom, Dad and I, and quite a few other passengers, stayed in the lounge far above the cabins, and at times, when the waves calmed down, we even ventured outside for some fresh air. While normally it was considered unacceptable, we even slept there. Under the circumstances, the captain looked the other way because due to the extreme stench of seasickness, going down to the cabins had become intolerable.

After a couple of days, we were out of the typhoon's reach, and returned to our cabin — our minds on our future life in Australia

Aside from these difficulties and general concerns, the majority of the month-long ocean trip was a pleasant experience. The Italian passengers were fun-loving, and, like the Hungarians, enjoyed life to the fullest. Our itinerary had taken us from Genoa across the Mediterranean through the Suez Canal, then south of India on the Indian Ocean. We stopped at the Island of Ceylon (now known as Sri Lanka), where we marveled at the beauty of the lush tropical setting, surrounded by groves of palm trees. We spent a lovely day sightseeing and ate lunch at the Mount Lavinia, a deluxe resort hotel, where we were pampered and treated like royalty. We felt guilty splurging, although it was the only day of the entire trip that we had the freedom to experience another culture. On a balcony overlooking the ocean, we sipped exotic drinks, and took in everything. Waiters and their helpers dressed only in sarongs showered us with deluxe service. This sort of treatment was strange to us, but, oh, so wonderful! After drinks, we were served our lavish lunch and reminisced about the many nights my parents had entertained our friends in Hungary. We kept thinking that life in Australia would not be easy at first; we would have to make lots of adjustments. But we were excited to get there, at last.

We arrived in Perth, Western Australia, and from there we traveled southward along the Australian Coast — finally arriving in Melbourne.

Chapter 25

LIFE IN AUSTRALIA

It was May 1957. My aunt, who had settled in Melbourne in 1951, invited us to stay with her and her family, but we soon felt we were intruding, despite their reassurances to the contrary. After a couple of weeks, we decided to move on to Sydney, where my uncle and grandparents lived.

Prior to leaving for Australia, my uncle had been a master baker in Vienna. Knowing that Sydney had more European immigrants than Melbourne, he decided to try his luck there. He started small, opening a retail store next to the bakery, which allowed the locals to become familiar with his wonderful bakery items.

In time, he became known for his delicious rolls, including the famous Austrian Kaiser roll, which fast became his signature product. Soon, customers wanted to enjoy them at restaurants, where they began requesting fancier breads. To satisfy their customers' demands, the restaurants bought their baked goods directly from him and his business grew into one of the biggest bakeries in Sydney.

Kaiser roll, some sprinkled with poppy seeds, others plain.   Delicious pastry

A single man, my uncle was renting a large apartment and insisted that we move in with him until we became more familiar with the city. There was a shortage of apartments in Sydney at the time, and the only way to get one was to put down a large deposit.

Our new life in Australia was hard. It meant getting used to a new language, new customs, and new people. Everything was foreign to us, and we spoke only a few words of English. The first weeks were particularly rough. We had to learn our way around the city, get used to heavy traffic, and adjust to driving on the left side of the street. At first, the simple act of crossing a street was a dangerous experience, because we always looked the wrong way.

New arrivals like us congregated at cafés in a European-influenced area of Sydney called Kings Cross. These cafés offered foods and other familiar trappings from the old countries, and as the demands grew, cafés expanded their menus to include a variety of favorite national foods. Hungarians, for example, were eager to enjoy gulyás (goulash), the typical Hungarian stew, as well as stuffed cabbage and an array of favorite desserts like strudel, chestnut puree, and palacsinta (Hungarian crepes).

Gulyás as a soup

Stuffed cabbage rolls

Prior to the 1950s, few immigrants entered Australia, but after the Hungarian uprising in 1956, a large influx of refugees arrived, bringing foreign attitudes, behaviors, and customs, which many Australians were reluctant to accept.

The situation changed, however, with the onset of American television. Many American programs showed the positive side of immigrants settling into new lives and assimilating into the American way of life. America's acceptance of newcomers helped Australians see both sides of the issue, and they began to accept, even appreciate and integrate, some European influences into their lives. At the same time, Europeans began to adjust to the Australian way of life. Always seeking acceptability, after acquiring Australian citizenship, they frequently took on more common English names. For example, my father changed our name from the Hungarian "Fekete" to "Black" — an exact translation. Fekete Gyorgy became George Black, Fekete Rozsi was now Rose Black, and Fekete Zsuzsanna became Susanne Black. In Hungary, last name comes first, followed by first name.

Like my parents, I had some difficulty getting used to our new life. Entering school was a big adjustment for me, and I didn't like anything about it. The school didn't offer foreign-born students any special assistance with the new language. I simply had to listen and absorb as much as I could. I attended regular classes and had to use the dictionary to understand the material and assignments. At first my progress was slow, but after a couple of months, suddenly everything began to click, and I became comfortable with English instruction.

I attended school with other immigrant children from various countries. Although we shared a European background, we did not share the same educational goals. Most of the others never handed in their homework assignments, they didn't ask questions, and their English did not seem to improve. I didn't like that sort of attitude and behavior, and after several weeks I asked my parents if there was any way for me to attend a different school. They decided that I would finish the school year where I was. During that time, I would vastly improve my English, so that I would be better prepared to transfer to a more difficult school at the start of the following year. The educational system in Australia was similar to Hungary's in that it was intensive, and the curriculum consisted of mainly compulsory subjects, with very few electives.

After an intensive search, my parents found a private all-girls school run by the Church of England and located in a lovely residential section of the city. They felt it was worth sacrificing everything and taking on the financial responsibility of high tuition. While very costly, they felt the importance of my participation in all the activities was essential to my integration into school life.

Summer school uniform   Winter school uniform

The education I received was wonderful, but I found it difficult to adjust socially. The school was filled with Australian girls who were not fond of non-Australians. My general behavior and formal manners were strange to them, and probably made them uncomfortable. They did not hide their dislike of me, and frequently made derogatory comments, which made me feel isolated and rejected.

Eventually, my relationship with my classmates improved a little, and school became more pleasant. But socializing on a personal level was quite another thing.

We needed more money, particularly to cover my school expenses, so my parents focused on learning enough English to buy a small café, which they expanded into a successful enterprise. The work was hard, but they were glad to have the opportunity and grateful to be free. It felt more like a blessing than a problem.

No matter how unwelcome we felt in Australia, we still appreciated being there. We didn't want to be Hungarians anymore; we wanted to integrate into the Australian way of life. Citizenship, which required a minimum of two years residency, was our next common goal. A couple of memorable incidents occurred during the swearing-in ceremony on September 26, 1959, my Dad's birthday. One of the government officials noticed his birth date, and, wanting to give him a special honor, asked if he would give a short speech. When the official returned to the podium, Mother asked Dad if he understood what the man had said. He did not. I had to explain to him that he had been asked to make a speech.

Dad was not a shy person, so, despite his minimal command of the English language, he figured he would be able to fake it somehow. We instructed him to say hello to everyone and to thank them for the opportunity to become a citizen. He agreed. The ceremony was lengthy with lots of speeches, and I had to go to the bathroom in the middle of the proceedings. As I was returning to my seat, I saw Dad already at the podium, and I suddenly felt anxious and embarrassed for him. I knew that he did not speak much English and I didn't want him to make a fool of himself. But he didn't seem to feel self-conscious at all. "I vant to sank you for zis honor and I am excited to become a citizen," he said.

I smiled, relieved; I hoped his accent had not taken away from the meaning. When I saw him bow to the crowd, showing his appreciation, my concerns turned to pride and guilt — I felt terrible for having doubted him. I should have known that he always found the right thing to say — and in his few words he expressed what he was feeling.

In December 1961, I was finishing up my school year at St. Catherine's and preparing for graduation. At the commencement ceremony, I was to receive a special honor in recognition of my scholastic achievements. I had come in second in my class, and the faculty realized this was a particular accomplishment for a student who had only been in the country for a few years. When my special honor was announced, everyone applauded and some of the parents congratulated me afterwards — but not any of my classmates. They may have resented me as a foreigner performing better than they did. Of course, my parents were proud and thrilled. They felt greatly rewarded for all their sacrifices. We had a big celebration in our apartment afterwards, to which we invited family and friends. Mom and I prepared all the food, which brought back many memories of the times she and I had spent together in the kitchen when I was a child.

After graduation, I had several choices regarding my future. In Australia, high school graduates may continue for one additional year of advanced studies and earn the equivalent of a college degree, which is referred to as "matriculation." This is followed by admission to schools of medicine, law or other career choices in higher education. I chose to complete this additional year. By now I was eighteen, and, instead of pursuing medical school and becoming a surgeon, which I always wanted to do, I decided that, for the time being, I would go to a business college. I took an intensive six-month course in secretarial skills such as typing, shorthand, business etiquette, and basic office procedures.

After graduation I began working as a secretary in a legal office for a group of patent attorneys. I had always been interested in scientific and technical work and was proficient in mathematics. Working in a patent attorney's office offered me access to many interesting technical concepts and reminded me of how important patents had been to my father's business in Hungary.

Given all of my negative social experiences at school, I never felt completely comfortable or at home in Australia. Not being able to fully integrate, I always wanted to travel. I wanted to experience new cultures, new people — new everything. But, feeling lonely, I was hoping to find a compatible friend with whom I could travel and discover new places.

Well, fortune smiled on me because within months of my mentioning it to my parents, they met a couple with a daughter my age. Coincidentally, Eva was also interested in going on an overseas trip. Even better, she had relatives living in Los Angeles who were delighted for the opportunity to welcome us into their home. It seemed like the perfect plan: a companion, a home to stay in, and an exciting destination. There was only one catch: my parents weren't thrilled about the idea of my traveling halfway around the world on my own.

Convincing them to let me go was not easy, but at least they were willing to listen. I gave them a number of good reasons, and they heard me — including the fact that many other young female graduates were traveling, especially to England, where they were able to work.

My parents always wanted the best for me and worked hard to provide it. They had sheltered and protected me all my life, so, of course, the idea of my being far from home worried them. Indeed, throughout my teenage years I often asked my mother why they were so protective of me. I knew that they trusted me, so why were they so worried? She always responded, "We feel more secure when you are near us." Now that I was older, they realized they had to give me more freedom. Only once during one of our many discussions did Mother reveal her deep feelings: she was uneasy and concerned when she wasn't sure of my whereabouts, and the thought of those terrible separations flooded her memory and made her ill with worry.

After finally convincing both sets of parents to support our dreams of traveling, Eva and I were finally ready to embark on a grand new adventure.

Chapter 26

LEAVING AUSTRALIA

Australia is called "down under" because it is so far from everywhere. The distance and the time it had taken us to get there fascinated me. Australia was the only Western life I had experienced, and I couldn't wait to see what America was like. Leaving was not only an adventure, but also a turning point for me. Being far away from my parents, seeing the world as an adult, and not knowing what was ahead for me — it was all so new and exciting. Eva and I bought passage to Los Angeles on the P&O Shipping Line's Canberra. We were to depart Sydney on February 10, 1963, on a twenty-one-day journey. To complete our trip to England, we also purchased passage on the SS France, traveling from New York to France in early October.

We were anticipating a thrilling voyage. Although I remembered my first experience on a ship, from Europe to Australia, to have its moments of disturbingly rough waters, I knew that this trip would be very different. This time, I was a young woman who had made my own decision to travel, and I intended to enjoy every aspect of it.

Some of the passengers were immigrating to the United States, while the majority of us were vacationers. Everyone spoke English and joined in the activities and festivities. Food and entertainment were available throughout the day and into the evenings. Eva and I found the other passengers pleasant, and enjoyed many interesting conversations and experiences.

On the day we left Sydney, the temperature registered 95 degrees with 100 percent humidity. Our own excitement added to the heat.

As the ship pulled out of port and Eva and I stood outside on deck waving goodbye to our families, our clothing stuck to us, and beads of perspiration trickled down our faces. Mine was mixed with tears. This was the first time in my young life that I had left my parents of my own choice. While I was excited about all the new experiences that lay ahead of me, I was sad for my parents, who were so kind and unselfish in letting me go.

Eva was a new acquaintance, and we had only paired up for the purpose of traveling together. She was a couple of years older, and that's really all I knew about her. Travel was our common ground. My feelings about leaving Australia were different from Eva's, and it was difficult for me to describe them to her. Having been born there, she had no knowledge of what we had lived through in Europe, or of my sense of alienation in Australia. I wasn't sure how much of it, if any, I should tell her.

Once our families were out of sight, Eva and I returned to our cabin, eager to freshen up. This departure from Australia marked a decisive step into adulthood.

Fresh from the shower, I went on deck, where I found a quiet spot of solitude to gather my thoughts and stare into the horizon. The calm ocean offered a much-needed peaceful moment of transition. Hungary, with all its hardships, deceptions, and lack of human rights; the unjust time spent in prison; our deportation; and the separation from my parents were all in the past. I had moved on and built an identity for myself in Australia.

During my years in Sydney, school and my workload were never a problem; only the lack of social life was difficult. English came naturally to me, and I spoke Hungarian only to my parents. I learned many Australian customs, disliked some, and readily adopted others. As I stood on the deck of the ship, I realized that yet another phase of my life lay ahead, and that now, more than ever, I must live in the present rather than the past. This time, however, I was in control.

I thought a great deal about my parents — how much they loved and protected me, and the hardships they had suffered in order to provide a good life in our newly adopted country. From the day I was born, they had sheltered me and were always by my side. Now, as Sydney Harbor faded into the horizon, I suddenly realized I was alone and without their security.

I was determined to keep in close contact with Mom and Dad and write to them every single day, keeping them well informed of my activities. Whether a letter, a card, or just a note, they would receive something each day from me letting them know how much they meant to me.

Along with my desire to keep my parents informed, I also wanted to feel like a grownup and able to stand on my own two feet. I never let anyone know how scared I truly felt. Imagining myself alone in the great, big world was a frightening thought, but experiencing it was even scarier. Every day there was something new to learn, and while the challenges were often overwhelming, they were also stimulating. I was definitely growing up and determined to make my own way.

Chapter 27

ARRIVING IN LOS ANGELES, AND LEAVING

Eva and I eagerly anticipated our arrival in the United States and talked about it much of the time. Upon our arrival, her distant relatives greeted us enthusiastically. They were incredibly generous, welcoming us with open arms and offering unlimited support. We could not have imagined better hosts.

The couple had never had children of their own, so they showered us with love and attention. They searched for interesting lectures, programs, and theatrical performances they thought would interest us. They even gave us one of their cars to use so we could discover the best of what the sprawling City of Los Angeles had to offer. Eva knew how to drive, and I took driving lessons. Within a couple of months, I got my license and we took turns driving around town. Every day was filled with wonderful new experiences, and I often felt like the luckiest person in the world.

After a while Eva and I were ready to part. She had met a young man and decided to stay in Los Angeles, so I contacted a friend in Sydney who I had heard was interested in traveling. As soon as Julie arrived in Los Angeles, we planned to head for New York together, where I was supposed to board another ship for a voyage to England.

In the meantime, I had contacted my friends in Hungary about their cousin Robert. This was the same Robert who was so nice to me as a little girl at that summer resort. He and his parents had escaped in 1956 after the Hungarian revolution and settled in Cleveland, Ohio, where they had relatives. As soon as I got their phone number, I called them and spoke to Robert's

mother, who told me that her son had just graduated from dental school and joined the U.S. Navy. He was stationed at Great Lakes near Chicago, prior to being assigned to a specific post. His mother suggested Julie and I visit him, and then go to Cleveland and stay with them.
I followed her advice, called Robert, and also accepted her invitation.

    Robert made arrangements with one of his colleagues to come into Chicago and spend the weekend there with Julie and me. On the first evening, while Julie fell asleep, Robert and I stayed up till three in the morning catching up, reminiscing about the old days. Although about nine years my senior, he and I had spent time together at the resort as children, and his parents and mine were friends — so we knew most of the people in their social circles. It was comfortable all these years later, just chatting with him. He knew something of what had happened to my family in Hungary and was interested in learning the details.

    We enjoyed the beautiful Chicago skyline, and just walking on Michigan Avenue was a thrill. Unlike Los Angeles, Chicago has a lot of beautiful, old buildings, including the magnificent white Wrigley Building. We ate at fun local places and followed dinner with long walks along the lake. It was such a cosmopolitan city, I felt at home right away. By the end of the weekend, Robert and I felt like old friends, and I was sorry to be leaving Chicago so soon.

    He had been very generous to Julie and me, especially since she was a complete stranger to him. During one of our conversations, he told me that in the Navy, well-shined shoes were a requirement, especially for officers. I had been wondering where to find a nice gift to show him our appreciation. Luckily, I found a beautiful shoeshine kit with a leather case, which I had monogrammed and sent to him prior to our departure. I was hoping it would arrive soon and that we would be able to talk again on the telephone once I arrived at his parents' home in Cleveland.

His parents, Gizi and Laci, greeted us warmly. The reminiscing I had done with their son now continued with them. It felt so satisfying.

One day, at the end of our first week's visit, Gizi was busy in the kitchen when the telephone rang, so I answered it. Robert was calling to rave about the lovely time he had spent with me on the previous weekend and asked to see me again. At that point, my plan was to leave Cleveland for New York with Julie and to catch the boat to Europe as originally scheduled. I had a visitor's visa due to expire within a few weeks, so we had to get on with our travel plans.

After my brief chat with Robert, I passed the phone to Gizi, who spoke to her son briefly, looked at me, smiled, and hung up. She took me aside and told me that during their conversation, Robert had said that he wanted to ask me to marry him, and was going to call back the next morning. I was shocked and speechless! It felt strange, and a bit funny.

The truth is that while we were in Chicago spending time together, I had entertained the idea of Robert as a potential husband, but during our conversations he had mentioned that he was in a long-term relationship.

Nevertheless, the strong connection we had formed over the weekend in Chicago was undeniable. After those two solid days with him, I came to realize how much we had in common. We came from similar backgrounds, our families knew each other well, and we had both left Hungary hoping for a better life in the West. With these similarities as a foundation, I felt that we had a good chance to build a life together. Robert had a good profession, he was gentle, and from our lengthy talks, I felt that he would make a great lifetime companion. I did not dare to dream too much, however, because I did not want to be disappointed. So, when Gizi told me the news, I was thrilled.

Next morning's telephone call from Robert was fairly short, yet we understood each other perfectly. He said he felt I was someone he had known for a long time, someone who shared his values and experiences, and could therefore understand him — just as I felt about him. We both felt that having so much in common gave us the best chance possible for a successful marriage. Remember, this was in 1963, and at that time many young couples based their decision to marry on shared values and goals, rather than on sexual attraction. Some still do. For these reasons, Robert and I felt very comfortable about becoming life partners.

Once we hung up the telephone, I sat there somewhat stunned, my mind racing in all directions. I wondered what to do about Julie, who depended on me as a traveling companion and would now be left alone — just like I had been in Los Angeles when Eva met her someone special. What would happen to our plans and to my passage to Europe? I hoped I would be able to get a cash refund. Then thoughts about a pending wedding flooded my mind. I was excited, exhilarated, and scared — all at once. And very importantly, thinking about my parents.

And just the thought of getting married! How could I organize it alone, without Mother, who was so far away? How would I handle all the details in a strange place? And what about after the wedding? Where would we live? After all, Robert was in the U.S. Navy and he might be sent somewhere far away on short notice. Where would I stay? What would I do? I had so many questions and very few answers.

When I had finally digested it all, I needed to call my parents but I had to wait for the right time due to the huge time difference. I didn't want to wake them up in the middle of their precious sleep. When I finally called, at about 7:00 a.m. their time, my father answered the phone. I asked him to get Mother on the extension so I could speak to both of them at the same time. He asked why, but by then Mom had picked up the phone. I blurted out my big news, and I asked them what they thought. I told them that I would accept the proposal only if they agreed to follow me to America. I said, "There is no way I could live here permanently without you."

I couldn't hear clearly everything they said, but a few sentences later I heard them express how happy they were to hear that instead of a stranger, my future husband would be someone they had known. After only a few more questions, they said, "Of course, we'll come! Your happiness is all that matters to us, and we gladly support your decision."

Plans came together, my parents arrived in time to help me prepare for the wedding, and the entire small family was present on the day Robert and I were married.

About two weeks earlier, Robert had received a relocation order from the U.S. Navy and was expected to report to Port Hueneme, California, for his next tour of duty.

A couple of days after the wedding on December 28, 1963, we left Cleveland and took up residence in Oxnard, near the Navy base, sixty miles north of Los Angeles. This was an amazing coincidence, because I was already familiar with Los Angeles.

Two months later, Robert was deployed to Guam to work at the dental clinic while his construction battalion of about 600 men was building roads and landing strips in Vietnam, including the Chu Lai Airfield.

On my way to visiting my parents in Australia, I spent a few months with Robert on Guam, and in October of 1964 we returned to the U.S., back to Port Hueneme. Since we decided to settle in the Los Angeles area, Robert had to take the California Dental Boards, which he passed on his first attempt.

In June of 1965, Robert received an honorable discharge from the Navy and we began our lives as civilians, residents of Beverly Hills. Robert opened a practice and we had a daughter, Michelle, now 54 with a family of her own — a son and a daughter.

At present, we live in Los Angeles, just a few minutes from our former Beverly Hills surroundings, and even now, 56 years later, we often chat about those magical moments we shared in Chicago. Most of all, we have never stopped being grateful for the opportunity to live in this great country, the United States of America.

EPILOGUE

Reflecting on our lives, we realize how invariably history repeats itself and that despite the passage of time, hatred remains a fundamental flaw of human nature.

Looking back to my early years in Hungary, I recall many traumatic incidents that left an indelible mark on my character. But every one of those experiences served as opportunities for growth, which, even now, helps me cope with challenging situations. I believe there is merit to the saying "Every cloud has a silver lining," and in the belief that overcoming harsh circumstances makes you a stronger, wiser, better person. Happier, too.

The most important lesson to learn from Destination Freedom is to never settle for a watered-down or slanted version of history that fails to represent a complete and accurate picture of events — of how and why they occurred, and their potential influence on our future. Based on what I witnessed as a child under Communism, I know the importance of leaving historical artifacts and monuments intact as symbols of pride or painful reminders, so that generations to come may learn from them and judge for themselves. In most school districts today, when history and geography are combined into a social studies curriculum, both subjects suffer the loss of essential material — further distancing us from the richness of our past — from its strengths, weaknesses, and guideposts for a better tomorrow.

Knowledge is power and can never be taken from you. So, seek out the knowledge of the past, as it is there you will find your best possible path to the future. I truly wonder, if you don't know your country's history, how can you love it? And, if you do know it, how can you hate it?

"The antidote to hatred, bigotry and anti-Semitism is education."

-- Pastor John Hagee

Despite the oppression and deprivation my parents endured, they had the will to keep their hopes alive. They always emphasized the positive and were able to instill in me that we can learn from every moment of hardship and use that knowledge to our advantage. Now, I am deeply aware that without adversity one cannot appreciate the good, and without hope there is no future. So, let my story inspire you to take responsibility for your own life and, when hardship comes your way, to never give up or give in.

I raised my awareness and respect for history by reading, looking at photographs, watching films, and discussing the atrocities directly with those people who also experienced them. Difficult a topic as it is, it took me several years to feel comfortable enough to talk about it.

My mission going forward is to raise awareness of both major oppressions that occurred in my lifetime — Nazism and Communism. In contrast to the Nazi era, there is considerably less information available and far less discussion on the suffering endured under Communist oppression — despite the duration and extent of their cruelty. With so much talk about socialism and communism in the news, it is important to be aware of the facts rather than accept information from biased sources. Listen to as many viewpoints as you can, and then make up your own mind. Often, it is not what is said that is important but what is left out. It is your task to know what is being left out, by whom, and why, and how to recognize it when confronted. It's a big chore to ask of your generation, but your future and safety depend on it.

If you take anything away from the lessons you learn from my story, it should be the often-quoted cautionary words of George Santayana:

"Those who cannot remember the past are doomed to repeat it.

"Of all forms of government today, only capitalism celebrates freedom. However, freedom is not free; it comes with responsibilities. We must respect it, treasure it, never take it for granted, and most of all, never abuse it.

I am grateful to have survived both Nazism and Communism and even more fortunate to live in this great United States of America. Teaching the next generations is my way of giving back. It is my greatest honor and pleasure to inform youngsters about oppression and atrocities during my lifetime so they can be better equipped to handle it.

Following my presentation to Kyle's class and other classes at his school, I received numerous messages of appreciation. So my mission to educate and inspire based on my life experiences has already gotten off to a good start. Although each child was affected by a different episode, they all came away enriched. They learned from a firsthand witness about life beyond their own. I will always treasure their thank-you notes and, most of all, hope they preserve the message of what I taught them.

"Dear Mrs. Reyto:

Thank you for coming to talk about your life. It was very interesting; I wish I could learn more about it. You should write a book about it. I think it would sell."

...

"I learned a lot and it reminded me of how lucky I am to live today without having to worry about being captured by Nazis or Communists."

...

"I will always remember what you said about people. Not all people are bad."

...

"I went home and told the story to my family; they were really interested and enjoyed it as well, but not as much as I did. I hope you can come back in a few years and talk to my little sister when she is in 8th grade."

...

"It taught me to be grateful for all the things I have in life. I do not take things for granted. I was on the edge of my seat the whole time. I kind of had an idea what it must have been for you growing up, but I learned a lot more."

...

"I am not Jewish but to learn about another person's perspective on something so evil is very cool. I could never survive something like that."

◆◆◆

As I am writing this, I cannot help but think about the events of September 11, 2001. You probably only heard about it; it happened when you were very young or not yet born. The twin towers in New York City were targeted by a pair of low-flying airplanes piloted by terrorists, and, within minutes, came tumbling down. Three thousand lives were lost in the disaster, and the event will forever affect us. The continued aggression by fanatics keeps reminding us of the evil forces in the world whose beliefs and goals differ radically from our own. Beyond any doubt, 9/11 was a turning point for everyone in the free world, but especially here in the United States, where foreign powers had never before unleashed such mass destruction. Many of us who had not thought about it previously woke up that day to the necessity of standing strong against the forces of oppression.

Early in 2020, the Covid-19 global pandemic brought forth another struggle for us to overcome. Its effect on our country was overwhelming. It caused us to make major adjustments to all aspects of our daily lives, including quarantine, which all but shut down our economy. Because we are social animals and interaction with friends and families is essential to our well-being, adhering and adjusting to "social distancing" became a major life-changer, even within family circles. Sporting events and cultural performances were abruptly suspended, restaurants were closed, barbershops and hair salons were shut down, medical and dental procedures — some important — were postponed indefinitely, and "going out" meant little more than taking a walk or a restricted trip to the market — in both instances, while wearing a mask.

As a result of this episode, some permanent changes will mark our lives going forward, as increasing numbers of classes will be made available online, various types of meetings will be held on Zoom, and other forms of business and entertainment will be conducted virtually.

However, the most important lesson the United States can learn from the pandemic is that we must no longer depend on other countries to manufacture our basic needs. This failed policy of recent decades points to our taking responsibility for our own interests. Our economy, the safety and welfare of our citizens, and our jobs market depends on it.

Those fortunate enough to have grown up in this freedom-loving country have never had to deal on a personal level with global adversity or confrontation with evil forces. Now, however, we are all too painfully aware that with hateful fanatics creating political unrest in our country and around the world, we must, more than ever, be vigilant about the potential dangers to our security and our cherished American way of life.

This chronicle of my journey from oppression to freedom demonstrates that a life dominated by hatred and persecution can turn into one of fulfillment. My late mother would be gratified to know she helped bring her story to the younger generation, so that they might learn from the ills of the past and, thereby, avoid their repetition. There were many stops, reversals, and obstacles along the way for my family, but the destination was worth everything. My parents' dream of coming to the West was the fulfillment of their years-long struggle to survive and their dream to raise me in freedom. Through sheer courage and determination, we reached our cherished goal. I am here to tell you, no matter the odds, it can be done and it is worth it.

Throughout my life, I always listened to and believed in my parents, and everything I learned I owe to them. Even when I was unhappy with their comments and expectations, I realized they meant the best for me. Their comforting, reassurances, and lots of pep talks made me the person that I am. Life is precious and experiences mold our lives. It is even more precious when you can share it with others. I hope you will learn from these life lessons and enrich your lives. In gratitude to those who helped and guided me, I dedicate my life to giving back by educating people to be informed citizens and to contribute to society.

The dictionary defines a dream as "something that somebody hopes or longs for — usually something difficult to attain." It is my dream that my experiences become the foundation for higher awareness, and a model for the human ability to rise above agony and misery and move ever forward, toward a greater destiny.

Freedom

is a precious commodity
and comes with responsibility.
We must protect, respect and cherish it,
not take it for granted,
and most of all never abuse it.

"Dream what you want to dream,
Go where you want to go,
Be what you want to be,
Because you have only one life
And only one chance
To do all the things you want to do."
~ Anonymous

◆◆◆

"Let your hopes, not your hurts, shape your future."
~ Robert H. Schuller

www.ingramcontent.com/pod-product-compliance
Lightning Source LLC
Chambersburg PA
CBHW062058290426
44110CB00022B/2630

Susanne M. Reyto is an award-winning author, speaker, world traveler, and an ardent supporter of Israel and the free world.

She works tirelessly for the preservation of our American way of life, liberty, and the education of our future generations about history.

Susanne is a child survivor of the Holocaust and grew up under Communism. Her childhood experiences and her ultimate escape from Communist Hungary in the late 1950s left Susanne with an unwavering spirit of optimism and perseverance. This is the message she spreads to audiences, young and old.
She grew up in Australia, lived on Guam while her husband served in the U.S. Navy, and has traveled the world.

Her writings have been featured in major U.S. newspapers and internet magazines and websites. She has appeared on television and radio in the U.S. and Canada. Her previous book, Pursuit of Freedom, has been designated as recommended reading for youngsters.

Her life today is balanced between family, business, cultural activities, and philanthropy. Susanne is married and has one daughter and two grandchildren. She and her husband make their home in Southern California.